MW01230635

THE SPIRIT WITHIN

*An Inquiry Into Humanity's Inner Spirit and
God's Communication With It*

Dr. Jon Robertson

© 2013 by Jon H. Robertson. All rights reserved.

No part of this book may be reproduced, stored in a retrieval system, or transmitted by any means without the written permission of the author.

Third Edition
Published by Petri House Publications

ISBN: 979-8-3669-2730-7

Library of Congress Control Number: 2013905569
Cover design by: Grouchy girls Collective
Photo Credit: Greg Rakozy

Because of the dynamic nature of the Internet, any web addresses or links contained in this book may have changed since publication and may no longer be valid. The views expressed in this work are solely those of the author and do not necessarily reflect the views of the publisher, and the publisher hereby disclaims any responsibility for them.

Dedicated to
my precious wife, Florence,
who inspired me to seek a deeper relationship
with the universal God,
and
to the Facts of Faith Christian Fellowship
for the opportunity to share His love.

ACKNOWLEDGEMENTS

This book is the outgrowth of a series of sermons that I preached on the spirit of humanity and its ability to partake of the divine nature to the Facts of Faith Christian Fellowship. Their response to these sermons inspired and encouraged me to attempt this written inquiry. Without the Fellowship's love and support, I doubt I would have undertaken this project.

A very special thanks should be given to Clarence Brown, whose editorial work and general advice had a profound impact on the final structure and content of this book, and to my son-in-law, Jonathan Phillips, Esq. whose attention to the detail and logic of writing was responsible for the final draft. I am also indebted to Dr. Alvin McLean and Dr. Lourdes Morales-Gudmundsson, whose theological critiques were invaluable. A special thanks is owed to Dr. Marc Christophe, Dr. Charles Teel and Dr. Diane Abdo whose insights have also profoundly impacted this work. I owe special thanks and gratitude to Lena Robin Berchielli, communications and marketing consultant, for her expertise in crafting and refining this work.

Table of Contents

Preface

As the son of a brilliant and powerful preacher and theologian, I grew up in a home devoted to the reading and study of the Bible. Wanting to be a student of the Word, like my beloved father, I found great delight in studying the Scriptures on my own.

Of great interest to me in my studies were the Hebrew Scriptures and God's intimate covenant relationship with one group of people—the Israelites. While I found this relationship fascinating and admirable, I began to question what God's relationship was with the rest of the world, and what His avenue of communication with them might have been. Surely, if John 3:16 is true and that "God so loved the world, that He gave His only begotten Son," to die for all humanity, then all peoples of the world—in every age—must have had access to his love in one form or another. For years this question weighed heavily on my mind, until the day I came across the passage of Scripture in Job 32:8 that read: *"But there is a spirit in man, and the breath of the Almighty gives him understanding."*[1] The simplicity and profundity of that statement seemed to be the answer to my questioning— *Throughout the ages, God dealt directly with every human being by communicating with their spirit.*

Of note, the Book of Job is arguably the oldest book in the Bible. It is a non-Judaic book, written in the Patriarchal Period approximately

---

[1] Unless otherwise noted, in-text Scripture citations refer to the New King James Version. *The Holy Bible* New King James Version (Nashville: Thomas Nelson Publishers, 1985).

2000 BC, and predates the Mosaic law by some 500 years.[2] In the opening chapter we see God's involvement in both earthly and universal matters (Job 1 and 2). For this reason, the statement, "But there is a spirit in man, and the breath of the Almighty gives him understanding", speaks directly to all of God's creation.

I was also curious about the distinction Scripture makes between our spirit and the Holy Spirit, and their joint work and relationship to the other existential parts of our being—the heart, mind and soul. In the Bible, we read that humanity was created in the image and likeness of God. This passage implies that God, like us, is tangible. On the other hand, we are told that God is a Spirit and can only be worshipped "in spirit" and in truth. This concept implies a mystical essence, devoid of shape or form. Thus, as humans, we face the dilemma of harmonizing the coexistence of the intangible realm of the spirit with the tangible material world.

An article by Vince Rause in the "Los Angeles Times Magazine", discusses the book, *Why God Won't Go Away*, with its author, eminent neuroscientist Andrew Newberg. The article explained that Dr. Newberg's hypothesis is, "that the brain's machinery of transcendence is set in motion by a mind willing itself toward the divine." His book describes experiments using SPECT (Single Photon Emission Computed Tomography) scanning the map the brain activity of both Tibetan Buddhists as they meditated and Franciscan nuns in deep prayer. The scans photographed variations in neural reverberation levels at the peak of each individual's contemplative state, activity which Dr.

---

[2]   Commentary on the book of Job, *The Holy Bible* New King James Version, (Nashville: Thomas Nelson Publishers, 1985).

Newberg and others believe indicate that "feelings [of mystical union with God] ... are rooted not in mere emotion, or wishful thinking, but in the genetically arranged wiring of the brain."

While Dr. Newberg and fellow scientists continue to engage in this investigational study, I would submit that the Creator *did* wire the brain to experience the tangible and efficacious power of God: *"But there is a spirit in man, and the breath of the Almighty gives him understanding"* (Job 32:8).

This inquiry is divided into two parts. *Part I* examines the methods by which God communicates with the spirit within, and explores the relationship to the other mystical parts of our being: mind, heart and soul. *Part II* seeks to explain how *this communication with God can,* in the words of Peter, *"make us partakers of the divine nature" through seven divine characteristics: virtue, knowledge, self-control, perseverance, godliness, brotherly kindness, and love.* The reader will note that following pages draw liberally from the Bible, as it is the greatest witness of the voice of the Almighty throughout the ages.

I sincerely hope that through this inquiry "seed thoughts" will be planted, enticing the reader to explore the unfathomable riches of God's wisdom and love. I further invite the reader to allow the Holy Spirit to speak to your *spirit within*, to guide and direct not only your spiritual thinking, but your daily lives. God's love has only deepened my conviction that He is able to convey His will to every human in every age. I pray that you will fully embrace the belief that there is "a spirit in man, and the breath of the Almighty gives him understanding" (Job 32:8).

PART I

Chapter I
John's Revelation

No one can come to Me unless the Father who sent Me draws him; and I will raise him up at the last day.

John 6:44

J ohn the Revelator, looking through the lens of God's prophetic telescope, witnesses an extraordinary spectacle:

> After these things I looked, and behold, a great multitude, which no one can number, of all nations, tribes, peoples, and tongues, standing before the throne and before the Lamb, clothed with white robes, with palm branches in their hands, and crying out with a loud voice, saying, "Salvation belongs to our God who sits on the throne, and to the Lamb!" Revelation 7:9, 10

This extraordinary vision should cause the reader to pause and reflect on the nature and scope of this innumerable host of diverse peoples, all acknowledging in a unified voice that the gift of salvation is the divine and exclusive domain of God, the Father, and His Son, the Lamb. The sweeping inclusiveness of the vast multitude must surely prompt one to question how all these peoples gained access to the glorious knowledge of salvation. Given the diversity of nations, the breadth of geography, and the vast sweep of time, I would suggest that the answer is either outrageously complicated or surprisingly simple.

When we consider that are races of people whose disappearance is still a mystery, and still others who have been victims of genocide, then it should be self-evident that somehow God's saving grace was offered to them during their lifetime. Even if our present technological capability to transmit information had existed during past eons, it would be a far stretch of reason to assume that the global population could be successfully reached solely through the preaching of the Gospel. In addition, the various belief systems and cultural mores that have existed from the earliest of times—along with the antagonism that adherence to such systems has often engendered— makes it unlikely that such a vast number of people could collectively embrace one universal God. Further, when we observe the religious wars fought in the past and present times, along with the exclusivity fostered by religious groups, John's vision becomes even more untenable to the rational mind. However, John's visions cannot be dismissed simply because of our difficulty in comprehending them. To the contrary, such should cause us to explore the Word of God prayerfully and seek a divine understanding.

Drawing Power

To begin our inquiry, we must explore the collective affirmation made in Revelation 7:10 by that innumerable host: "Salvation belongs to our God who sits on the throne, and to the Lamb!" This statement unequivocally declares that God and His Son, the Lamb, are responsible for our salvation. Note the order here: God the Father is positioned before His Son the Lamb—intentionally. While we are accustomed to the concept that Jesus brings us to the Father, it is in fact the loving Father who gave us "His only begotten Son, that whoever believes in Him should not perish but have everlasting life" (John 3:16). Consequently, this supernal gift of the Father places Him at the forefront. Jesus Himself offers the keys that unlock the door to our understanding of the Father and His work: "No one can come to Me [Jesus] unless the Father who sent Me draws him" (John 6:44).

This passage begins to explain why the Father logically precedes the Son in John's prophetic vision. Without the drawing power of the Father, it is impossible for anyone to come to Jesus, or to salvation. Let's take a moment to ponder the importance of this operative word "draw." Draw is defined as: "To cause to move in a given direction by applying continuous force ... or to a given position, as by leading."[3]

This definition implies that the person or object to be drawn may exhibit some resistance, thereby requiring either continuous force or some form of enticement. Draw also describes a process by which one moves from one state or place to another. The word "draw" speaks to the Father's relentless desire to succeed in His quest. Since Jesus Himself is explaining the work of His Father, there can be no argument as to its validity. Jesus continues: "It is written in the prophets, 'They shall all be taught by God.' Therefore, everyone who has heard and learned from the Father comes to Me" (John 6:45).

Consider these words carefully: "they shall all be taught by God." Keep in mind what Jesus revealed to Nicodemus, a leading Pharisee and teacher in Israel: that God so love *the world*, and that He demonstrated His love in the sending of His Son. Therefore, the phrase, "they shall all," must refer to all nations, tribes, peoples, and tongues. The statement declares God has endeavored at some point in time to reach every person in the world! The second sentence however, makes an important exclusion for some: "Therefore everyone who has heard and learned from the Father comes to Me." "Heard and learned" speaks to a conscious desire on the part of the listener to hear and understand what is being said and then to respond. We

---

[3]   "Draw," *The American Heritage Dictionary*, 3rd ed. 1994.

must recognize that *choice* is a prerequisite for salvation. *God cannot draw or save anyone against their will.* Only when one *chooses* to learn from the Father can the drawing process be actualized. Here, Jesus elucidates:

> All that the Father gives Me will come to Me, and the one who comes to Me I will by no means cast out. For I have come down from heaven, not to do My own will, but the will of Him who sent Me. This is the will of the Father who sent Me, that of all He has given Me I should lose nothing, but should raise it up at the last day. And this is the will of Him who sent Me, that everyone who sees the Son and believes in Him may have everlasting life; and I will raise him up at the last day.
>
> John 6:37-40

From a casual reading, Jesus' statements about the Father's will may appear redundant; however, they speak to separate but equally important ideas. The first "will" speaks holistically to all peoples throughout the ages who did not see the Son, but came to believe as a result of the Father's drawing. The second "will" speaks specifically to those Jews and Gentiles who literally saw the Lamb (Jesus), the fulfillment of the promise, and believed in Him. Thus, the innumerable host as seen by John was composed of both those who had personally seen Jesus, as well as those who believed without seeing Him.

Another important fact is that the plan of redemption was in effect *before the foundation of the world* (Ephesians 1:4). The host of saints who never saw Him rose from their graves at the resurrection of Jesus. Matthew 27:52, 53 records that a tremendous earthquake caused some graves to be opened and many of the saints that had died in the precious hope of the resurrection were raised, went into the city, and appeared to many.

John in his epistle makes clear that the *light of divinity has touched every individual that has ever lived.*

> In the beginning was the Word, and the Word was with God, and the Word was God. He was in the beginning with God. All things were made through Him, and without Him nothing was made that was made. In Him was life, and the life was the light of men ... That was the true light which gives light to every man who comes into the world. * John 1:1-4, 9

The words "gives light to every man who comes into the world," confirm an inclusive act of God in reaching all peoples. Peter gives supporting evidence of God's will to save all humanity, underscoring how God is "long suffering towards us, *not willing that any should perish* but that all should come to repentance" (2 Peter 3:9).

---

* Original italics have been removed from all Scriptural quotations, as they do not confer emphasis but rather refer to alternative manuscript sources. Thus, any italics used have been added by the author for emphasis.

Chapter 2
Unconditional Love

For I am persuaded that neither death nor life, nor angels nor principles nor powers, nor things present nor things to come, nor height nor depth, nor any other created thing, shall be able to separate us from the love of God which is in Christ Jesus our Lord.

Romans 8:38, 39

T he Scriptures identify a bold process by which God draws us to Him. The primary drawing force is *unconditional love,* which causes an awakening of our *faith*, leading us into *repentance and finally into submission.* In this and subsequent chapters, we will explore this process and how God uses each of these stages—love, faith, repentance, and submission—in unique ways to draw us into a relationship with Him.

A Special Love

First and foremost, in this process is unconditional love—that divine attraction that causes us to "love Him because He first loved us" (1 John 4:19). Indeed, the human need to love and to be loved is a powerful motivating force. Every facet of our being responds to it. When children are reared with an abundance of love, there is a sensitivity and warmth that underscores their character. Conversely, the *lack* of love is equally evident and is largely responsible for much of the dysfunctional behavior we experience in today's world. Considering how favorably we respond to *human love*, how much greater then should our response be to the powerful drawing of the *agape*, the divine love of God. It is this unique *agape* - or divine unconditional love - which Jesus was referring to in His Sermon on the Mount (Matthew 5-7).

The truths and concepts Jesus preached must have been unfamiliar to the multitudes that came to hear Him. He taught them to love their enemies, give a blessing to those who cursed them, show goodness to those who hated them and, most appalling of all, pray for those who spitefully hurt and persecuted them. Jesus further taught that His Father's love was constantly shown by His making the sun rise on both the good and the evil, and sending the rain to both the just and the unjust. Loving only those who love you does not reflect God's love.

Human behavior seems to function on the principle that we love those who do good and show indifference or scorn to those who do evil. So, when we see God's goodness showered upon both the just and the unjust, we may question His fairness. We must understand that the concept of God's unconditional love ignores good and evil as a condition for loving. *Be perfectly clear, however, that unconditional love does not condone evil; rather, it demonstrates God's divine nature in that He can love the sinner while condemning the sin.* To love the sinner but not the sin is possible because God *is* love. God did not wait until we "exhibited goodness" before He demonstrated His ultimate expression of love towards us. It was *while* we were at our absolute worst that He died for us!

If, when we were under sin's control, God unconditionally showered us with love, how much more awaits us when we respond and return our love to Him? (Romans 5:6-11).

Love in Action

In teaching the multitudes about God's love and concern for humanity, Jesus presents three parables about the joy of finding something valuable that was lost. Often Jesus used different metaphors to express the same idea. In so doing, He could reach a diverse crowd by giving them the opportunity to identify with at least one of the parables. The first parable is about a lost sheep. Jesus, being sensitive to the economic realities of ownership, knew the value placed on each animal. We should also keep in mind that, on other occasions, Jesus had identified Himself as the "Good Shepherd" who had come to save the "lost sheep" of the world. Therefore, the significance of this metaphor is profound.

> What man of you, having a hundred sheep, if he loses one of them, does not leave the ninety-nine in the wilderness, and go after the one which is lost until he finds it? And when he has found it, he lays it on his shoulders, rejoicing. And when he comes home, he calls together his friends and neighbors, saying to them, 'Rejoice with me, for I have found my sheep which was lost!' Luke 15:4-6

"I have found my sheep which was lost!" This personal identification and willingness to seek the lost, regardless of where they may be, shows the unconditional nature of God's love. Like all great teachers Jesus interprets the parable by giving its true meaning, lest anyone miss the point. "I say to you that likewise there will be more joy in heaven over one sinner who repents than over ninety-nine just persons who need no repentance" (Luke 15:7). We saw earlier that it is the Father who draws us to Jesus. Here, we see Jesus'

commitment that, once drawn to Him, he will not let us stray- "of all He has given Me I should lose nothing" (John 6:39).

The second of the three parables is most interesting for, unlike the first or third parable where men are used as the metaphor for God seeking the lost, a woman is now the protagonist seeking the lost. During Christ's time, when women were of a low social and economic status and were not often used as positive role models, this parable must have created a strong sense of identification for the many women present.

> Or what woman, having ten silver coins, if she loses one coin, does not light a lamp, sweep the house, and seek diligently until she finds it? And when she has found it, she calls her friends and neighbors together saying, 'Rejoice with me for I have found the piece which I lost!' Likewise, I say to you, there is joy in the presence of the angels of God over one sinner who repents. Luke 15:8-10

The third parable is without question the most powerful and descriptive of the three. The prodigal son, who requests and receives his inheritance from his father, leaves home to live a riotous life, squandering all his inheritance. Finding himself desolate and in a foreign country, he takes a job feeding swine. Remembering that in his father's home even the servants ate well, he comes to his senses and returns home a broken man. Before he can deliver his prepared repentance speech, we read:

> But when he was still a great way off, his father saw him and had compassion, and ran and fell on his neck and kissed him.   Luke 15:20

God running to fallen humanity, in our most depraved condition, embracing and kissing us, speaks volumes not only to the unconditional love of God, but to His love in action. These parables, as spoken by Jesus, represent the heart and soul of divinity's desire to save the lost of the world. The intensity and persistence in finding the lost in each parable should bolster our faith in God's love for every individual.

Chapter 3
Faith

But without faith it is impossible to please Him, for he who comes to God must believe that He is, and that he is a rewarder of those who diligently seek Him.

Hebrews 11:6

O nce the power of unconditional love is recognized, faith is required to gain a deeper understanding of that love. "Now faith is the substance of things hoped for, the evidence of things not seen" (Hebrews 11:1). From this passage, we can clearly discern that faith is mystical. Divine energy brings actualization or substance to things we hope for, and allows belief based on evidence of things we cannot see. The word "faith" must, therefore, be reserved for spiritual application only. We apply this word to our everyday routine far too casually. For example, the analogy, "It takes *faith* to fly in an airplane." Not really. You may need *courage* to fly, but not faith. Such a statement does not meet the faith litmus test. First, the plane can be *touched*, while faith is the substance of things hoped for. Second, the plane can be *seen*, while faith is the evidence of things not seen. Finally, proven *physical* laws all but guarantee the plane's ability to fly, while faith, in its essence, is mystical. *Faith is God's divine wind beneath our spiritual wings.*

Mystical Reality

How then is faith an important element in the "drawing" process? The unequivocal answer is found in Hebrews: "But without faith it is impossible to please Him, for he who comes to God must believe that He is, and that He is a rewarder of those who diligently seek Him" (Hebrews 11:6). Herein lies the all-important condition: "must believe that He is." Faith materializes God to our understanding and brings conviction—without doubt—of His existence and power. The last clause of this text, "and that He is a rewarder of those who diligently seek Him," shows belief as motivating our *choice* for allowing the Father to draw us to His Son. *Once the drawing process gains momentum, we shift from our being drawn, to a proactive desire on our part to diligently seek Him.* So, the function of faith is both to activate our belief in the Father and the Son, and to motivate our participation in the drawing process.

How do we obtain faith? One begins by acknowledging that "faith is divine" and not human (as pointed out in our airplane example). Consequently, faith can only be dispensed by the Divine. Further, it is logical to reason that since we grow from "faith to faith" (Romans 1:17) we must start with a measure of faith. Paul confirms this: "For I say, through the grace given to me, to everyone who is among you, not to think of himself more highly than he ought to think, but to think soberly, as God has dealt to each one a *measure of faith*" (Romans 12:3). This measure of faith is actually "seed faith," which the Father cultivates to initiate the drawing process. Just as a small amount of water is used to prime a pump, the measure of faith primes our capacity to believe and trust God and to follow His leading in our lives.

Paul addresses the means by which we further acquire faith—through the hearing of God's voice. "So, then faith comes by hearing, and hearing by the Word of God" (Romans 10:17).

Notice that Paul does not say hearing *of* the word of God, but rather hearing *by* the word of God. This nuance is in concert with the words of Jesus when He speaks of humanity *hearing and learning* from God the Father: "It is written in the prophets, 'And they shall all be taught by God' therefore everyone who has heard and learned from the Father comes to Me" (John 6:45).

If an increase of faith came simply through the hearing *of* the word, then all who have for years heard the word preached should have attained great faith. *Preachers must remember that while they are privileged to preach the gospel, it is still the voice of God through the Holy Spirit that indites hearts and brings revelation to our inner spirit.*

Our individual capacity to express faith may differ from one to another—similar to talents or intelligence. But rest assured that every individual has the basic capacity to believe and accept the gift of salvation. Too often, we pit one individual's faith against another's, causing conflict and despair. Faith is not intended to be competitive or comparative. To the contrary, faith is designed to enrich our individual relationship with God and to share with others the miraculous power of divinity. Paul encourages us to act in accordance with the degree of faith given.

Having then gifts differing according to the grace that is given to us, let us use them: if prophecy, let us prophesy in proportion to our faith; or ministry, let us use it in our ministering; he who teaches, in teaching;

he who exhorts, in exhortation; he who gives, with liberality; he who leads, with diligence; he who shows mercy, with cheerfulness.
Romans 12:6-8

Faith in Action

How can this theory be practically applied? The Scriptures offer innumerable examples of the drawing power of faith. Let us consider three different vignettes through which we can vicariously feel the pull of God's Spirit. Notice how each individual's divine encounter not only resulted in answered prayer, but, more importantly, how it instilled within each one a deeper revelation of God Himself.

The first vignette is about the healing of the woman with a terminal blood disease. We find her broken and discouraged.

Now a certain woman had a flow of blood for twelve years, and had suffered many things from many physicians. She had spent all that she had and was no better, but rather grew worse. When she heard about Jesus, she came behind Him in the crowd and touched His garment for she said, "If only I may touch His clothes, I shall be made well." Immediately the fountain of her blood was dried up, and she felt in her body that she was healed of the affliction. And Jesus, immediately knowing in Himself that power had gone out of Him, turned around in the crowd and said, "Who touched My clothes?"

But his disciples said to him, "You see the multitude thronging you, and you say, 'Who touched me?'" And He looked around to see her who had done this thing. But the woman, fearing and trembling, knowing what had happened to her, came and fell down before Him and told Him the whole truth. And He said to her, "Daughter, your faith has made you well. Go in peace, and be healed of your affliction." Mark 5:25-34

From this account, we do not know much about the depth of this woman's spiritual experience. We do not even know if she initially thought Jesus to be the Son of God. We do know that she recognized Him as a Divine Healer, and that her faith in His divine power *drew* her to reach for His garment. We see here, a classic example of faith in operation: she presumably had seen or heard of Christ's healing powers; she envisioned her own healing; and, most importantly, she sought out the Lord and reached out to Him. Her faith drew her to the feet of the very One who would freely give not only physical, but spiritual healing - a profoundly greater blessing than she could have possibly imagined.

Consider another spectacular demonstration of faith:

Now when [Jesus] concluded all His sayings in the hearing of the people, he entered Capernaum. And a certain centurion's servant, who was dear to him, was sick and ready to die. So when he heard about Jesus, he sent elders of the Jews to him, pleading with Him to come and heal his servant. And when they came to Jesus, they begged him earnestly, saying that the one for whom he should do this was worthy, for he loves our nation, and has built us a synagogue.

Then Jesus went with them. And when he was already not far from the house, the centurion sent friends to Him, saying to Him, "Lord, do not trouble yourself, for I am not worthy that you should enter under my roof. Therefore, I did not even think myself worthy to come to you.

But say the word, and my servant will be healed. For I also am a man placed under authority, having soldiers under me. And I say to one, 'Go', and he goes; and to another, 'Come', and he comes; and to my servant, 'Do this,' and he does it." When Jesus heard these things, he marveled at him, and turned around and said to the crowd that followed Him, "I say to you, I have not found such great faith, not even in Israel!" And those who were sent, returning to the house, found the servant well who had been sick. Luke 7:1-10

These two accounts illustrate that universality of the faith dynamic, which **transcends any one denominational dogma**—and "church" membership is clearly not a prerequisite. Here we see again the inclusiveness of the drawing process: on one hand, a Jewish woman, and on the other, a Roman Gentile. The centurion, like the woman, had probably observed Jesus in other settings and recognized divine qualities in Him. By beholding, he was drawn to experience that special power that he had seen at work for so many others. The result was nothing less than remarkable: a Roman soldier daring to believe that Christ could heal from a distance, sight unseen. Christ Himself marveled at such belief - especially from a Gentile - noting that, "I have not found such great faith, not even in Israel" (Luke 7:9).

The final profile of faith is, without question, the most unusual and controversial of the three examples. The central character is certainly not from the Jewish "moral majority", or any other respected class of society, but rather from the absolutely lowest of all social strata. This unlikely heroine is none other than a prostitute, whose bravery and resolute faith spared her life, and that of her entire family, when Joshua's army set out to overtake Jericho. While hiding Joshua's spies in her home, she was questioned by representatives of the king of Jericho. She acknowledged the spies' visit, but said she had no idea where they went after leaving her. She then encouraged the king's men to pursue the spies quickly. The story becomes particularly interesting at this point, as one perceives a clearer sense that this prostitute, Rahab, is being *drawn* to a spiritual awareness of God's power and ability to save her household. She tells the spies that she knows that "the Lord your God is God in heaven above and on earth beneath" (Joshua 2:11). Rahab enters into a pact to save herself and her family when Joshua's men return to take the land. As agreed, she placed a scarlet cord in the very window they had used to escape. On the seventh and final day of Joshua's vigil, the walls of Jericho fell to the sounds of trumpets and the shouts of Israel's army. But what happened to Rahab?

> And Joshua spared Rahab the harlot, her father's household, and all that she had. So, she dwells in Israel to this day, because she hid the messengers whom Joshua sent to spy out Jericho. Joshua 6:25

What a marvelous display of faith in the God of heaven and earth, and in His power both to destroy and to save. Rahab's response to God's *drawing* power led her to a new state of spiritual awareness and ultimately to her salvation. Moreover, in what could be considered the ultimate tribute to Rahab's phenomenal display of faith, God honored her as one of *only two women* inducted in the *Faith Hall of Fame* in Hebrews 11. She forever ranks side-by-side with such spiritual giants as Abraham, Sarah, Isaac, Joseph, Moses, Gideon, Samson, Samuel, and David. And to allay any questions as to whether this was indeed the ill-reputed Rahab, whom skeptics of our time might find too objectionable to share such august ranking, the writer of Hebrews began his salute with this unmistakable description: "By faith the harlot Rahab did not perish with those who did not believe, when she had received the spies with peace". Hebrews 11:31

The power and ministry of faith exhibited by all three of these individuals should inspire us to press forward despite the seemingly hopeless and painful circumstances. Paul encourages us with this statement:

> Therefore, we do not lose heart. Even though our outward man is perishing, yet the inward man is being renewed day by day. For our light affliction, which is but for a moment, is working for us a far more exceeding and eternal weight of glory, while we do not look at the things which are seen, but at the things which are not seen. For the things which are seen are temporary, but the things which are not seen are eternal...For we walk by faith, not by sight. 2 Corinthians 4:16-18, 5:7

Chapter 4
Repentance

The Lord is not slack concerning His promise, as some count slackness, but is long suffering toward us, not willing that any should perish but that all should come to repentance.

2 Peter 3:9

Repentance has been a significantly misunderstood concept. Notions of contrition taught over the last two millennia have been a breast-beating state of brokenness in which we agonize over our past sins and enter, as it were, into a never-ending state of self-flagellation. This teaching is no more than a cruel exchange of crippling guilt for the self-imposed prison of penance. For purposes of this inquiry, repentance may be defined as the willingness to atone for our misguided deeds, or as the commitment to personal accountability and integrity in our relationship with God. When considering the concept of repentance, the reader may interchangeably use the term "contrition" for his or her human failing.

Repentance is the desired and beneficial outcome of the drawing (or inviting) process of unconditional love and faith. Often, repentance is viewed as being one-dimensional—a recurring act of confession. Confession is an acknowledgment of wrongdoing. On its own, though possibly cathartic, and sincere, confession is incomplete, in that it requires no further responsible action. Therefore, confession is only a step toward repentance.

A clarifying example of the incompleteness of confession without repentance is the admission of, then repetition of, unhealthy choices or wrongdoing, even while feeling anxiety and guilt about that choice. *Repentance involves the commitment to, and demonstration of, consciously, or purposely, eliminating unhealthy or negative behaviors from our choices of action.* True repentance says, "Not only was I wrong, but I'm deeply sorry for it, and by God's grace I am determined not to do it again." In this contrite state, we have effectively made the critical turn leading to the foot of the cross. There, God accepts our repentance and showers us with divine forgiveness. *The fact is that repentance is far more than just asking God for forgiveness, it is our gateway to a personal relationship with Him.*

The work of the Holy Spirit to awaken us to our need for repentance and to instruct us in the consequences of straying from the wisdom of God's will. Peter reminds us that both repentance and forgiveness are gifts from God (Acts 5:31). Because we are inherently self-centered and bent on doing what seems right to us, our natural inclination, of course, is to reject the Spirit's leading. Through varying life experiences - both good and bad - the Spirit convicts us of God's truth and continually encourages us to accept this liberating pardon and salvation. Continual resistance to His encouragement results in inner conflict. (Paul, in Romans 7, portrays it as *warfare!*)

At first reading, - to give both repentance and forgiveness may seem strange. However, a spiritual equation explains why both repentance and forgiveness come from God. *With God, the quality of forgiveness must equal the quality of repentance.* How meaningless forgiveness would be if, for example, our repentance was only cosmetic at best, or insincere at worst.

We return to the parable of the prodigal son as a further example of true God-given repentance and forgiveness. After squandering his inheritance in wasteful living, the prodigal finds himself destitute in a foreign country in the midst of a famine. He finds a job as a feeder of swine, but his employer will not feed him or even allow him to share some of the carob pods he feeds to the swine. At this point we see the *drawing* power of repentance at work, causing him to evaluate his condition. We read: 'but when he came to himself'; these profound words represent his entrée to repentance. Repentance begins once we sincerely confront ourselves, cease the game playing and self-justification and take full responsibility for our condition. This act of repentance enables us to put things into their proper perspective. He continues:

'How many of my father's hired servants have bread enough and to spare, and I perish with hunger. I will arise and go to my father, and will say to him, "Father, I have sinned against Heaven and before you, and I am no longer worthy to be called your son. Make me like one of your hired servants." (Luke 15:17-19)

Two points are important in his resolve. First, he understands that repentance to God that must precede any earthly request for forgiveness. Second, realizing that he made poor choices, he is now willing to humble himself. Therefore, true repentance is synonymous with true humility. One cannot negotiate with God for true repentance. The next sequence of events reveal the quality and sincerity of the prodigal son's repentance.

"And he arose and came to his father. But when he was still a great way off, his father saw him and had compassion, and ran and fell on his neck and kissed him." Luke 15:20

His father, seeing him from a distance, throws caution and reserve to the wind, and, demonstrating overwhelming compassion, embraces his son, even in his filthy condition, and kisses him. Surely, the father's demonstrative reception might have indicated to his son that all was well and that he could hope to be restored to his former status. But listen to the prodigal:

> "And the son said to him, 'Father, I have sinned against Heaven and in your sight, and I am no longer worthy to be called your son.' Luke 15:21

No statement could be greater proof of the quality of his repentance before God and man. The quality of the father's forgiveness is equal to the quality of his son's repentance. Note the father's response:

> "But the father said to his servants, 'Bring out the best robe and put it on him, and put a ring on his finger and sandals on his feet. And bring the fatted calf here and kill it, and let us eat and be merry; 'for this my son was dead and is alive again; he was lost and is found'. And they began to be merry." Luke 15:22-24

Since God, through the Holy Spirit, *draws* us to repentance, His forgiveness in like quality is guaranteed. Jesus reminds us of a similar equation in the prayer He taught to His disciples. We read "and forgive us our debts, as we forgive our debtors." (Matthew 6:12) In fact, His forgiveness is contingent on our forgiveness of others. "For if you forgive men their trespasses, your heavenly Father will also forgive you. But if you do not forgive men their trespasses, neither will your Father forgive your trespasses." (Matthew 14:15)

Only through repentance can we begin to experience the full warmth of God's unconditional love. Truly, if one has tasted of repentance and the overwhelming response of God's pardon, then one knows firsthand the transformational sense of liberation—freedom from guilt and discouragement, freedom from internal conflict, and, yes, freedom from sin's grip and control over our lives.

Chapter 5
Submission

Therefore submit To God. Resist the Devil *And He Will Flee From You.*

James 4:7

A s powerful and essential to our salvation as repentance is, the act is merely a gateway to the final stage of the drawing process—*submission to (or surrender to)* God. In this sacred space, God establishes a life-changing relationship with us. Here God comes down and meets us as we are. In this "inner sanctum" we are eligible to be partakers of His divine nature.

Like repentance, submission has also been misunderstood. Religious establishments have portrayed submission as a state of powerlessness, as punishment for misdeeds or ego-based thoughts or actions. No wonder the idea of submission to God is shunned like the plague. While submissive sinners *do* experience profound contrition and "godly sorrow" for their sins (Corinthians 7:10), they do not leave the foot of the cross feeling spiritually bludgeoned and devalued. Instead, they are revived, reconciled, and restored into fellowship with God through trust in His love. Once we submit to, or trust in, His divine love, we are accorded all of the graces necessary to *enjoy* life and to "have it more abundantly" (John 10:10).

Humility is the defining quality in submission to God. We abide, walk, and talk with God, as did David when he penned these immortal words of comfort:

The Lord is my shepherd; I shall not want.

He makes me to lie down in green pastures;

He leads me beside the still waters.

He restores my soul;

He leads me in the paths of righteousness for His name's sake.

Yea, though I walk through the valley of the shadow of death,

I will fear no evil; for You are with me.

Your rod and Your staff, they comfort me.

You prepare a table before me in the presence of my enemies;

You anoint my head with oil; my cup runs over.

Surely goodness and mercy shall follow me all the days of my life;

And I will dwell in the house of the Lord forever. Amen.

Psalms 23

This Psalm is, without question, one of the most beloved passages of all Scripture. Each verse exudes the Shepherd's love and protection, and brings consolation and peace to the reader. Of note are the overpowering benefits that are guaranteed the submissive individual:

1. Freedom from want
2. Restorative leadership
3. No fear of death
4. No fear of evil
5. Protection and comfort
6. Anointment by God
7. His divine mercy

Having the guarantee of such benefits must bring consolation and peace. However, in the beautiful metaphor of the Shepherd, He requires that we become as submissive as sheep. Somehow, being submissive does not appeal to our independent, assertive natures. *In our culture, nothing is inviting about the prospect of becoming a docile, defenseless creature.* A lion, a fox, a bear maybe...but certainly not a sheep! And, what really is the underlying problem with regarding yourself as a sheep? Who wants to release control? We well know that the Shepherd metaphor requires us to do what our natures resist most—giving up control of our will and allowing God to Shepherd and lead us in *all* facets of our lives.   Jesus elaborates on this Shepherd/sheep relationship:

"Most assuredly, I say to you, he who does not enter the sheep fold by the door, but climbs up some other way, the same is a thief and a robber. But he who enters by the door is the shepherd of the sheep. To him the doorkeeper opens, and the sheep hear his voice; and he calls his own sheep by name and leads them out. And when he brings out his own sheep he goes before them; and the sheep follow him, for they know his voice. Yet they will by no means follow a stranger, but will flee from him, for they do not know the voice of strangers." Jesus used this illustration, but they did not understand the things which He spoke to them. Then Jesus said to them again, "most assuredly, I say to you, I am the door of the sheep. All who ever came before me are thieves and robbers, but the sheep did not hear them. I am the door. If anyone enters by Me, he will be saved, and will go in and out and will find pasture." John 10:1-9

How reassuring! The sheep, which the Father *draws* to Jesus, cannot be deceived by strangers nor those who would do them harm. The Shepherd's flock learns to recognize His voice. The sheep listen and obey. They find comfort in the Good Shepherd's words: "I am the door, if anyone enters by Me, he will be saved, and will go in and out and will find pasture" (John 10:9). The knowledge that the evil one cannot terrorize or imprison us gives us comfort. We know where to find the green pasture of peace. Christ says: "other sheep I have which are not of this fold; them also I must bring, and they will hear My voice; and there will be one flock and one shepherd" (John 10:16). There is one Shepherd, and there is one flock—representing all nations, tribes, peoples, and tongues.

There is a divine promise that is inextricably tied to submission. "Humble yourselves in the sight of the Lord, and He will lift you up." (James 4:10) Pride is the enemy of humility and for that reason we are warned "God resists the proud, but gives grace to the humble. Therefore, submit to God. Resist the devil *and he will flee from you*" (James 4:7).

The promise of God's grace makes submission (or surrender) a glorious state. We receive all of the benefits and privileges of Christ's atoning sacrifice on the cross at Calvary, the awesome peace that transcends all human understanding, and the joy of feeling reconciled with God.

Moreover, repentance and submission come with a value-added promise from Jesus: "Come to Me, all *you* who labor and are heavy laden, and I will give you rest. Take My yoke upon you and learn from me, for I am gentle and lowly in heart, and you will find rest for your souls. For My yoke is easy and My burden is light." (Matthew 11:28-30) Truly, submission is not an experience to be shunned; rather it is to be *celebrated* in humility as the most desired of all spiritual experiences.

Chapter 6
The Spirit Within

But there is a spirit in man, and the breath of the Almighty gives him
understanding.

Job 32:8

e have covered much ground in exploring the various ways and the
extraordinary lengths to which our God will go to bring us into
fellowship with Him. We have examined His *"drawing"* process
and the glorious state of submission we can experience after responding to
Him through repentance. We reveled in the realization of God's grace and His
Son's righteousness. God's mystical work of sanctification begins within us.
The Holy Spirit works through our spirit to recreate, reshape, and restore us
to God's image. This life-long process takes place at the deepest spiritual level.

The Spirit with a Small "s"

Let us begin then by exploring this experiential notion of the "spirit
within." We gain some initial insight through a statement made by Elihu, a
young protégé of Job who declares: **"But there is a *spirit* in man, and the *breath*
of the Almighty gives him understanding"** (Job 32:8). Two operative words are
worth noting here: "spirit" and "breath". Let us consider "spirit" first. **Notice
that "spirit" is characterized by the lowercased "s" and refers to our *human*
spirit in contrast to uppercased "S" of the Holy Spirit.** This difference is

critically important to understanding the interactive dynamics between the two, which we will explore later. The Hebrew word for "spirit" is *ruwach*, literally meaning "wind" or "breath." Additionally, its meaning refers to a metaphysical entity that is rational and capable of expression and function.[4] The "wind" metaphor should remind us of Jesus' private conversation with Nicodemus in which He explained the "born again" phenomenon: "The *wind* blows where it wishes, and you hear the sound of it, but cannot tell where it comes from and where it goes. So is everyone who *born of the Spirit*" (John 3:8). *Interestingly, in the New Testament, the Greek word for "spirit" and "Holy Spirit" is "pneuma", which is translated as "wind" or "breath", as is the Hebrew word "ruwach" in the Hebrew scriptures.[5]*

Certainly, we do not think of the Holy Spirit as solely "divine air" but as the ultimate mediator of God's will and power. *In like fashion, the spirit that is within cannot be viewed simply as the "breathing of air," but rather as a communicator that can receive inspiration and instruction from God.* This "inner spirit" concept that Jesus espoused was incredibly confusing to Nicodemus, who considered himself a religious scholar and one of God's elect. "How can these things be?" he asked. And Jesus' poignant reply was even more riveting: "Are you the teacher of Israel, and do not know these things?" (John 3:9, 10)

The notion that we actually commune with God through the spirit within is reinforced through yet another of Jesus' private conversations - this one with a Gentile woman from Samaria. In this dialogue, Jesus also exposes a startling revelation about the way we should worship.

---

[4]   James Strong, Dictionary of the Hebrew Bible, 1890, 107. New Strong's Exhaustive Concordance of the Bible, (Nashville: Thomas Nelson Publishers, 1984).

[5]   James Strong, Dictionary of the Greek Testament, 1890, 58. New   Strong's Exhaustive Concordance of the Bible, (Nashville: Thomas Nelson Publishers, 1984).

The woman said to Him, "Sir, I perceive that you are a prophet. Our fathers worshiped on this mountain, and you Jew say that in Jerusalem is the place where one ought to worship."

> Jesus said to her, "Woman, believe me, the hour is coming when you will neither on this mountain, nor in Jerusalem, worship the Father. You worship what you do not know; we know what we worship, for salvation is of the Jews. But the hour is coming, and now is, when the true worshipers will worship the Father in spirit and truth; for the Father is seeking such to worship Him. God is Spirit, and those who worship Him must worship in spirit and truth. John 4:19-24

Here Jesus introduces the "church without walls," a highly radical (even heretical) concept for a religious society whose dogmas, temples, and synagogues were considered the only gateways to God. Much to the woman's surprise, Jesus - being a "Jew and prophet" - declares that a structure or setting for worship is not as important to God as is the way we must worship Him - in spirit (small "s") and truth. *Communing with God through our inner spirit is indeed the ultimate form of worship.* And since it comes from within, we can engage God anywhere we physically find ourselves.

This inward spirituality refers back to Jesus' conversation with Nicodemus, which revealed that the spirit world is also God's domain, often transcending religious structures and conventions. This realization facilitates our fundamental understanding that God the Father and His Son are Spirits, as is the Holy Spirit. Their domain is where the cosmic struggle is being played out between good and evil spirits vying for the occupancy of our souls. Paul notes: "For we do not wrestle against flesh and blood, but against principalities, against powers, against the rulers of the darkness of this age, against spiritual hosts of wickedness in the heavenly places" (Ephesians 6:12). Thus, the spirit that God plants within each of us—along with the indwelling Holy Spirit—also protects us from being controlled by evil forces.

God's Breath

Having examined the "spirit" aspect of Elihu's statement, let us now look at the other concept: "and the *breath* of the Almighty give him understanding" (Job 32:8). Derived from the Hebrew word, neshâmâh, "breath" means a "puff" or "wind," "divine inspiration" or "intellect".[6] The most applicable definitions in this context are, of course, *inspiration and intellect.* From this, we see how God communicates with us and how the interactive dynamic of the spirit and breath actually works. So, through God's "breath of inspiration", we have the ability to individually understand His will for us. Such inspiration channeled through our inner spirit puts us on God's divine frequency.

For what man knows the things of a man except the *spirit* of the man which is in him? Even so no one knows the things of God except the *Spirit* of God ...

> These things we also speak, not in words which man's wisdom teaches but which the Holy Spirit teaches, comparing spiritual things with spiritual. But the natural man does not receive the things of the Spirit of God, for they

---

[6] Strong, *Dictionary of the Hebrew Bible, 81.*

are foolishness to him; nor can he know then, because they are spiritually discerned. But he who is spiritual judges all things, yet he himself is rightly judged by no one. For "Who has known the mind of the Lord that he may instruct Him?" But we have the mind of Christ. 1 Corinthians 2:11, 13-16

To see God's inspiration at work, one need only consider the events surrounding the birth of Jesus. The Son of God was born in Bethlehem to the amazement of a few shepherds, who were told of the miracle by angels. Some two years later, an entourage from the East appeared before Herod's gate, bearing expensive gifts for the "King of the Jews" whom they had come to worship (Matthew 2:2). The question arises: how did these "wise men" learn of this event? Let us say, for argument's sake, that some Jewish missionary traveled to the East, teaching that the birth of Jesus would occur sometime in the future, or that a manuscript of Isaiah was made available to the Magi. These men still required the breath of the Almighty's inspiration, coupled with extraordinary faith, to motivate them, *Gentile* dignitaries, to follow a star across the dangerous desert for nearly two years to worship the babe they called "King of the Jews." After paying homage, the Magi are again inspired, to return by a different route, thereby foiling Herod's scheme to find and kill the Christ Child. The account also demonstrates how God's inspiration flows to everyone who will receive it, irrespective of one's religious persuasion or level of intellect. *God always communicates in terms and vocabulary we individually understand.*

I am sobered by the fact that this divine form of communication between God and humanity has been downplayed in traditional Christianity, if not completely ignored. *You can imagine the profound impact on our society if adults, as well as children, were taught that God has placed within us a spirit, that still small voice that guides our actions in all activities, and teaches us to discern right from wrong. Knowing that we all possess this inner spirit, we gain a better understanding of its purpose to make us the people God intended us to be.*

Chapter 7
The Function of the Spirit and the Heart

Create in me a clean heart, oh God, and renew a steadfast   spirit within me.

Psalms 51:10

N ow that we have investigated the spirit within, we can explore its functions as it relates to God's perfecting work. We will first expand on God's process of *drawing* us to the glorious state of submission (Chapter 5) and into a saving relationship with Him. Solomon, purported to be the wisest man who ever lived, gives us an unequivocally clear picture of the function of this spirit. In Proverbs, he notes: *"The spirit of a man is the lamp of the Lord, searching all the inner depths of his heart"* (Proverbs 20:27). Nothing could be more self-explanatory. **Our inner spirit is God's lamp—or searchlight—into our hearts.** Not by accident or by chance, but by design (see Preface). Our Creator, in His infinite wisdom and foreknowledge of human nature and all its propensities, designed us with an internal mechanism—the lamp. He uses this light to: 1) expose our inner character to us; 2) reveal our need for His guidance along life's journey; and 3) ultimately draw us into a covenant relationship with Him. Let us now further consider why God places within us a spirit to search the inner depths of our hearts.

Divine Anatomy

The *heart* is the repository of our emotions (*e.g.,* love, hate, anger, peace). The *mind* is the seat of our intellect (*e.g.,* reasoning, knowledge and understanding). Of the two, the heart would appear to be more powerful. We have only to look at our own experiences to witness the power of emotions over reason. How many times do we reason through and settle on, a particular course of action—clearly deciding the rational thing to do—only to cast it aside when the emotions of the situation take charge? How many times have we found ourselves unable to understand our intense feelings—positive or negative—about a certain person or situation? And how many times have our emotions caused us to say or do things impulsively, only to regret them later? Our emotions, when not guided by Godly love and understanding, can lead us to dark places.

God says only He can understand the carnal heart: "I, the Lord, search the heart, I test the mind, even to give every man according to his ways, and according to the fruit of his doings" (Jeremiah 17:10). David, who understood this well, cried out: "Search me, oh God, and know my heart; try me, and know my anxieties; and see if there is any wicked way in me, and lead me in the way everlasting" (Psalms 139:23, 24).

Jeremiah recognized the worst potential of the emotional heart— "deceitful above all things, and desperately wicked; who can know it?" (Jeremiah 17:9). By asking the sobering question: "Who can know it?", Jeremiah implies that one cannot truly *trust* the emotional heart. Surely, this must be the reason God warns us to place our trust in Him and not in ourselves or in each other, particularly in these days of wavering ethics and deteriorating values.

Should we be surprised at the heart's potential for evil when we consider the origins of sin? Isaiah takes us back to those dark days when sin took root in the heart of "the most beautiful" angel, the prince of the most heavenly host.

> How you are fallen from heaven, oh Lucifer, son of the morning! How you are cut down to the ground, you who weaken the nations! For you have said in your heart: I will ascend into heaven, I will exalt my throne above the stars of God; I will also sit on the mound of the congregation on the farthest sides of the north; I will ascend above the heights of the clouds, I will be like the Most High.   Isaiah 14:12-14

Lucifer nurtured in his *heart* a burning desire to be like God - if not to *become* God. When he beheld his own beauty, his covering of precious stones, and the pipes and timbrels in his throat, his desire turned to pride (Ezekiel 28). Pride led to obsession and ultimately to rebellion. His consuming lust for divinity and his efforts to usurp God's throne ignited war in heaven that led to his ouster (Revelation 12:7-9). The virus that attacks our hearts, as it did Lucifer's, is *temptation.* James enlightens us on our own propensity to sin by exposing the lure of temptation.

> Let no one say when he is tempted, "I am tempted by God"; for God cannot be tempted by evil, nor does He Himself tempt anyone. But each one is tempted when he is drawn away by his own desires and enticed. Then, when desire has conceived, it gives birth to sin; and sin, when it is full-grown, brings forth death. James 1:13-15

Temptation is unique to each individual. We are not all *tempted* by the same things or in the same way. What is an overpowering temptation for one individual, may elicit no response in another. Rightly understood, temptation is, at best, a *strong suggestion*, which of itself has no power over us, unless it finds resonance in our own desires. Once the temptation finds a response in us and has been *conceived*, we have effectively sinned in thought. Beyond that, it is only a matter of time and opportunity for the act to be carried out.

Thankfully, a spiritual antidote can effectively attack the temptation virus and render it impotent. Scripture calls it *"submissive resistance"*: *"Submit to God. Resist the devil and he will flee from you"* (James 4:7). Under the pressure of temptation, God offers His all-sufficient grace (power) which enables us to stand in *divine* strength and *resist* even the most potent temptation: "Therefore take up the whole armor of God, that you may be able to withstand in the evil day, and having done all, to stand. Stand therefore, having girded your waist with truth, having put on the breastplate of righteousness" (Ephesians 6:13, 14).

Jude, in his time-honored doxology, assures us that we serve a God whose grace is not only sufficient to pardon us, but, able to empower us to overcome temptation's lure: "Now to Him that is able to keep you from stumbling, and to present you faultless before the presence of His glory with exceeding joy, to God our Savior, who alone is wise, be glory and majesty, dominion and power, but now and forever. Amen" (Jude 1:24, 25).

Now the fundamental question: is our emotional heart condition indeed curable? David prescribes the only effective procedure that can remedy our condition, and that is a *total spiritual heart transplant.* He understood this need when he entreated God to: "*Create* in me a clean heart ... and renew a steadfast *spirit within me*" (Psalms 51:10). David wisely asked God to renew the spirit within so that it would keep his new spiritual heart accountable and illuminate the right path. Keep in mind, this spiritual heart surgery requires a process of time. Therefore, we must be patient with ourselves, and most assuredly with others, as God performs this delicate and often painful spiritual procedure of surrendering to Spirit—but resplendent joys await us as the result of this renewal. Then we can join the psalmist David and say:

> My heart is steadfast, oh God, my heart is steadfast; I will sing and give praise. Awake, my glory! Awake, lute and harp! I will awaken the dawn. I will praise you, oh Lord, among the peoples; I will sing to you among the nations. For your mercy reaches unto the heavens, and your truth unto the clouds. Be exalted, oh God, above the heavens; let your glory be above all the earth. Psalms 57:7-11

Chapter 8
The Function of The Spirit and The Mind

And be renewed in the spirit of your mind, and that you put on the new man which was created according to God, and in righteousness and true holiness.

Ephesians 4:23, 24

T he relationship between our spirit and our mind is most fascinating, for it serves to link the third member of the Godhead - the Holy Spirit - to the extraordinary plan of salvation. Before we explore this, we must understand the role of the mind in our total metaphysical composition and how straying from the love of God has affected it. Paul has unfortunate news for us in this regard, similar to the frailties of the emotional heart as explained in the previous chapter. Consider our natural state of mind:

> For those who live according to the flesh set their minds on the things of the flesh, but those who live according to the Spirit, the things of the Spirit. For to be carnally minded is death, but to be spiritually minded is life and peace. Because the carnal mind is enmity against God; for it is not subject to the law of God, nor indeed can be. So then, those who are in the flesh cannot please God. But you are not in the flesh but in the Spirit, if indeed the Spirit of God dwells in you. Now if anyone does not have the Spirit of Christ, he is not His. Romans 8:5-9

Paul makes a clear distinction between our natural or *carnal mind* and the *spiritual mind* under the control of the Holy Spirit. And note that, without qualification, he affirmatively declares that only the *spiritual mind can please God*. This declaration invites some very troubling personal questions: Am *I* pleasing God? What is the state of *my mind*—carnal or spiritual? How does one *become* spiritual? These probing queries set the stage for us to consider the interactive work of the spirit and the mind. Remember that our inner spirit belongs to God. This embedded sensor, or "lamp" *per se*, that searches out the delinquent heart (see Chapter 7). This same lamp can also be used to shed the light of truth on our carnal minds.

Paul formulates an argument to show not only the work of the spirit within, but also the work of the Holy Spirit—and the similarities between the two: *"For what man knows the things of a man except the spirit of the man which is in him? Even so, no one knows the things of God except the Spirit of God"* (1 Corinthians 2:11). Paul presents a profound equation: *our spirit is to us what the Holy Spirit is to God*. Our spirit searches and knows all things about us, just as the Holy Spirit knows all things about God. Paul suggests *there is an interactive relationship between our inner spirit and the Holy Spirit, and our mind and the mind of God*.

> But as it is written: eye has not seen, nor ear heard, nor have entered into the heart of man the things which God has prepared for those who love Him. But God has revealed them to us through His Spirit. For the Spirit searches all things, yes, the deep things of God. For what man knows the things of a man except the spirit of the man which is in him? Even so, no one knows the things of God except the Spirit of God. Now we have received, not the spirit of the world, but the Spirit who is from God, that we might know

the things that have been freely given to us by God. These things we also speak, not in words which man's wisdom teaches but which the Holy Spirit teaches, comparing spiritual things with spiritual. But the natural man does not receive the things of the Spirit of God, for they are foolishness to him; nor can he know them, because they are spiritually discerned. 1 Corinthians 2:9-14

The Need for a Divine Relationship

The Holy Spirit mentors our spirit, revealing the spiritual things of God as they pertain to our daily lives and salvation. The unclean heart (which is driven by destructive emotions) and the carnal mind (which is contrary to God's love) find symbiosis. Every human emotion requires a plan to realize its intended desire. Your mind must devise a plan to satisfy your emotion. With careful planning, an emotion such as hate or anger can produce a heinous crime such as the September 11, 2001 terrorist attacks on the World Trade Center and the Pentagon. The emotion of jealousy or envy can lead one to devise plans to discredit others. The power of the carnal mind is best witnessed in the global destruction we see daily, as greed and ambition are executed with unerring precision. When we observe the evil of addiction to various substances, and the organized efforts to ensure its spread throughout the world, we have to be appalled. The cunning ability of the carnal mind is amazing. How often have we seen a project earmarked to do good for society become the vehicle of con artists who line their pockets with ill-acquired funds, or the desecration and burning of churches, temples, and mosques along with waves of child abductions, molestations, and murders? These atrocities have created a climate of fear and intimidation that often leaves the innocent paralyzed. We need no further evidence that *the human mind is in grave need of a divine makeover, which is the exclusive work of the Holy Spirit in partnership with our inner spirit.* Paul confirms this:

> But you have not so learned Christ, if indeed you have heard Him and have been taught by Him, as the truth is in Jesus: that you put off, concerning your former conduct, the old man which grows corrupt according to the deceitful lusts, and be renewed in the spirit of your mind, and that you put on the new man which was created according to God, in righteousness and true holiness. Ephesians 4:20-24

The revelation of God's mind to us gives perception to individuals who are "born of the Spirit". By this spiritual perception, one is able to visualize the hereafter while functioning at peak efficiency in the present world. Our whole perspective on life changes, as beautifully expressed in the well-known chorus of the hymn, "Turn Your Eyes Upon Jesus": *"Turn your eyes upon Jesus, look full in His wonderful face and the things of earth will grow strangely dim in the light of His glory and grace."*[7] This revelation also serves to empower our faith, to the extent that spiritual things become more easily discerned. The clouds of doubt that caused vacillation in our past between good and evil choices are blown away by the refreshing winds of the Spirit. With a renewed spirit, we become instruments of God's peace that enlightens the troubled world and brings hope to the hopeless. Now we can personally appreciate the promise of the New Covenant: "I will put my law in their (spiritual) minds, and write it on their (cleansed) hearts; and I will be their God and they shall be my people" (Jeremiah 31:33).

---

7   Helen H. Lemmel, "Turn Your Eyes Upon Jesus," 1992.

Yet another dimension to the relationship between the spirit within and the Holy Spirit—is the role of inner *witnessing*. Consider Paul's explanation: "The *Spirit* Himself *bears witness* with *our spirit* that we are children of God, and if children, then heirs—heirs of God and joint heirs with Christ, if indeed we suffer with Him, that we may also be glorified together" (Romans 8:16, 17). Take careful notice that the Holy Spirit witnesses *with*—not only *to*—our spirit. *What greater evidence can be offered that the spirit within and the Holy Spirit are communicative entities, capable of jointly witnessing.* Surely, to suggest, as some in Christendom have, that our inner spirit is merely our "breath" is unbiblical. If this were so, we would have to make the same evaluation of the Holy Spirit—as being only the "breath" of God—since Paul likens one to the other. Paul here confirms that the spirit within and the Holy Spirit bear witness that *we are children of God!*

In a letter to the church of Galatia, Paul speaks of the results of a cleansed heart and a spiritual mind; he calls them the fruit of the Spirit:

> But the fruit of the Spirit is love, joy, peace, long-suffering, kindness, goodness, faithfulness, gentleness, self-control. Against such there is no law. And those who are Christ's have crucified the flesh with its passions and desires. If we live in the Spirit, let us also walk in the Spirit. Galatians 5:22-25

Whenever I read this passage, I am always impressed with the fact that Paul speaks of only one fruit - not *fruits* - of the Spirit. The Spirit produces in each of us a life of godliness that bears a single fruit with these eight divine attributes:

1. *Divine love* for all humanity, regardless of color or status.
2. *Divine joy* in our lives regardless of problems or circumstances.
3. *Divine long-suffering* (patience), not only with ourselves but also with each other.
4. *Divine kindness*, which gives us understanding and sensitizes us to the needs of our society.
5. *Divine goodness* that abiding sense of what is right and just.
6. *Divine faithfulness* to be a guarantor of our word to God and each other.
7. *Divine gentleness* that caring and warmth that gives hope to all with whom we come in contact.
8. *Divine self-control* a balanced temperament that brings calm in the midst of chaos.

All of these divine attributes of the Spirit are *character traits - not doctrinal beliefs*. Religious doctrine and rules - fueled by human will power - may alter our behavior to some degree, but they are powerless to create renewed lives that reflect the true nature of the spirit-driven life. Nor can they produce salvation, or make us more pleasing to God. Living and walking in the Spirit is, in fact, a total lifestyle.

Paul admonishes:

> For he who sows to his flesh will of the flesh reap corruption, but he who sows to the Spirit will of the Spirit reap everlasting life. And let us not grow weary while doing good, for in due season we shall reap, if we do not lose heart. Therefore, as we have opportunity, let us do good to

all, especially to those who are of the household of faith.
Galatians 6:8-10

Isaiah offers a wonderful prescription to secure our spiritual being: "You [God] will keep him in perfect peace, whose mind is stayed on You, because he trusts in You" (Isaiah 26:3). A mind that is stayed on God is a mind equipped with divine shock absorbers. The bumps and potholes in the road of life are mysteriously absorbed. While others are distressed and panicking, those who have their minds *stayed* on God exhibit a divine peace, and "nothing causes them to stumble" (Psalms 119:165). *This reaction* is the result of spiritual-mindedness—the only state in which we are *in a relationship with God*. When you allow God's Spirit to witness with your inner spirit, that *you* are indeed His child, you receive within your renewed mind the Father's ultimate affirmation: *"You are my beloved child in whom I am well pleased."*

Chapter 9
The Function of The Spirit and The Soul

Love the Lord your God with all your heart, with all your   soul and with all your mind. This is the first and great commandment.

Matthew 22:37, 38

Materializing ethereal things, and compartmentalizing the spirit, heart, mind, and soul, as if they were visible parts of the body, can be difficult. Yet the Scriptures discuss each of these facets of human reality in a concrete manner. In this chapter, we will explore the soul, the last of the four aspects of our immaterial being. Biblical writers used the word "soul" liberally to describe different aspects of a person. For example, "soul" sometimes refers to "people" in general: "Then those who gladly received his (Peter's) word were baptized; and that day about three thousand *souls* were added to them" (Acts 2:41). Other times, "soul" is used to name that part of our being that connects on an emotional level with others: "And it was so, when he had finished speaking to Saul, that the *soul* of Jonathan was knit to the soul of David, and Jonathan loved him as his own soul" (1 Samuel 18:1). This connection can also operate on the divine level: "As the deer pants for the water brooks, so pants my *soul* for You, oh God" (Psalms 42:1). For the purpose of our inquiry, we will focus on a more specific definition of "soul" - that immaterial part within us that belongs to God, (Ezekiel 18:4) returns to Him at death (Genesis 35:18) and reigns with Christ. (Revelation 20:4)

An Eternal Record

In Deuteronomy, God admonished Israel to study and keep His commandments as He showered His love, mercy, and goodness on them. In this account, we gain clearer insight into the soul:

> Therefore, you shall lay up these words of mine in your heart and in your soul, and bind them as a sign on your hand, and they shall be as frontlets between your eyes. You shall teach them to you children, speaking of them when you sit in your house, when you walk by the way, when you lie down, and when you rise up. Deuteronomy 11:18, 19

Note the phrase; "lay up these words of mine in your heart and soul." To *lay up words* in the *heart and soul* is to keep a record of God's wisdom and instruction to us. We then keep these words in our hearts for daily living, and store them in our soul as a permanent record.

Therefore, we understand that, the Holy Spirit communicates with our heart (emotions) and mind (intellect), but within the soul God's divine truths, teachings, blessings, knowledge and power are stored (or saved). From this soul-based storehouse, the psalmist, David, repeatedly intoned, "Bless the Lord, oh my soul, and all that is within me, bless His holy name." This prayer is an example of David's understanding that his soul held, or stored, the messages and wisdom from the Spirit of the Almighty.

This storehouse of divine spiritual truths is the place within us from which our spirit communes at the deepest levels of understanding with the Holy Spirit in meditation, prayer, and worship. From our soul's depth we give praise and, in return, receive immeasurable blessings, one of which is divine peace that surpasses all understanding. The sanctity of the soul must be guarded at all times, for therein lies our spiritual treasure, a resting place for God within us.

Not only does the soul have the capacity to store God's knowledge, love and power; it has the unique ability to enlarge what is stored within. Listen to Mary, the mother of Jesus, prophecy to her cousin, Elizabeth, about the Son of God who is within her womb: "My soul *magnifies* the Lord, and my spirit has rejoiced in God my savior...and His mercy is on those who fear (respect) Him from generation to generation." (Luke 1: 47, 50) To magnify is to make larger the knowledge, power, love and blessings of God the Almighty. This message cooperates with Moses' words of wisdom in the Book of Deuteronomy (written over a thousand years earlier in approximately 1405 BC). Here, God's words to humanity come with a detailed approach to living. Most importantly, He instructs us to "teach them (His instructions for living) to our children".

Generational investment of God's word instilled our children ensures that future societies to come will be filled with adults who are attuned to the leading of the Spirit's wisdom in all aspects of their lives. God's love and blessing are given to counter the evil that permeates our society on every level of the economic and cultural spectrums. God instructs us to converse with the family in continuous dialogue of the blessings of the Spirit's ministration of God's love. This dialogue should occur in the home, as we travel in our daily routine, as we meditate and before we sleep. As a result of this continuous connection with God's love, we will surely find renewal of the Spirit's energy and wisdom as we wake to the challenges of a new day.

As a point to reflect upon, please notice that Mary's message to her cousin Elizabeth, about the importance of reverence of God through successive generations, was communicated around the year One BC. Fourteen hundred years earlier, circa 1405 BC, Moses emphasized the same concept of the importance of generational teaching of God's love and blessings, as they are stored in the soul (Deuteronomy 11: 18, 19). *Clearly, similar, and sacred beliefs and teachings by the Spirit of the Almighty have been delivered throughout time through different messengers. These beliefs, teachings and messages from God do not waiver over time or circumstance. To my mind, this evidence is incontrovertible; the unceasing efforts of the Almighty's Spirit speaks to the soul of mankind throughout the ages.*

The Spirit Within

Having first explored the inner working of the Spirit within our immaterial being, we have now observed how this extraordinary process provides us a spiritually fulfilling relationship with our God. The following seven points represent the perfection of grace through faith. Let us consider again this glorious process:

1. The *unconditional love* of the Father that draws (invites) us.
2. The path to Him through *faith, repentance (or contrition)*, and the glorious state of *submission (or surrender)*.
3. The *spirit within* that is guided by God.
4. The *cleansed heart.*
5. The *renewed spiritual mind.*
6. The *soul* that is inscribed with the Word of God.
7. The *renewing power* of the Holy Spirit in our lives.

My sincere prayer is that we all receive and embrace—heart, mind, spirit, and soul—the knowledge and understanding that comes from the breath of the Almighty who promises to make us whole and restored through His unconditional love.

Part II

Chapter 10
Partakers of The Divine Nature

His divine power has given to us all things that pertain to life and Godliness, through the knowledge of Him who called us by glory and virtue, by which have been given to us great and precious promises, that through these you may be partakers of the divine nature, having escaped the corruption that is in the world through lust.

Second Peter 1: 3, 4

In the preceding chapters we have studied how God reaches all people in every age through the spirit that is within. We have explored the miraculous drawing power of God's unconditional love, our access to Him through faith, and the indescribable divine peace that comes when we enter the gates of repentance and reside in the gracious mansion of submission. We have investigated the inextricable relationship of our spirit with our mind, heart, and soul, and, most importantly, the bonding of our spirit with the Holy Spirit to jointly witness that we are heirs and joint heirs of God.

Now, we will explore the message of the Almighty to the spirit within and various applications of this understanding to daily living. The intention of Part II of this inquiry is the ongoing development of the *"seven virtues"* within the reader, leading all toward a life filled with the connection with the spirit within. Moving forward, we will further explore the most glorious reality that Peter introduces in his second epistle: namely that, *believers, in their earthly life, may be actual partakers, or takers in part, of God's divine nature.*

The afterlife is often thought of as the point in time when we will finally become at one with God's nature. We have already seen in Paul's "fruit of the Spirit" analogy the possibility of living a life on *earth* that is pleasing to God (as noted in Chapter 8). Indeed, Jesus Himself, in His final prayer for His disciples, is focused on the importance of the earthly life: "I do not pray that you should take them out of the world, but that you should keep them from the evil one" (John 17:15). Jesus further adds, in looking to the future:

> "I do not pray for these alone, but also for those who will believe in Me through their word; that they all might be one, as You, Father are in Me, and I in You; that they also may be one in Us, that the world may believe that You sent Me." John 17:20, 21

I believe that while Jesus was praying for all of His disciples, two of them must have weighed heavily on His heart. First, Judas, who would sell his soul to the devil for thirty pieces of silver in a foolish betrayal of his Lord; and secondly, Peter, who betrayed his Lord only to become *sifted like wheat* (or tempted) by Satan (Luke 22:31). Hence, the testimonies of Peter are so powerful. No other disciple better embodies the transition "from sinner to saint."

Every individual should rejoice as they contemplate the life of Peter, a foul-mouthed fisherman, boastful and proud, who was nevertheless a natural leader. Peter, whose spiritual sensitivities would reach such immeasurable heights that, feeling unworthy to die in the same manner as his Lord, he requested to be crucified upside down. As he contemplated his imminent death, Peter beseeched believers to partake of the divine nature, as he did, encouraging us to be "neither barren nor unfruitful in the knowledge of our Lord Jesus Christ" (2 Peter 1:8).

Partaking of the Divine nature is the true meaning and purpose of the drawing power of the Father. No doubt, this offering is what Paul calls, "our epistle written in our hearts, known and read by all men" (2 Corinthians 3:2).

The Invitation

Peter addresses his letter to the church to "those who have obtained like precious faith with us by the righteousness of our God and Savior Jesus Christ" (2 Peter 1:1). Peter is inviting those of faith to join in his experience. I pray that those on this spiritual path would thank God for His patience as He waits for our growing faith to embrace His power and love. God understands that at some point all have been in doubt, where we partially believe but cry out from our unbelief. Peter's invitation further promises that the knowledge of God the Father, and His precious Son Jesus will multiply grace and peace within us.

Attempts at spiritual growth apart from that of God's Spirit, such as through adherence to religious dogma or exclusive belief systems, often, at best, produce self-righteousness. We must also accept that divine love, or "salvation", cannot be found merely through an academic searching of the Scriptures. Jesus's confirmation of this statement must have knocked His detractors off their feet, "*you search the Scriptures, for in them you think you have eternal life; and these are they which testify of Me. But you are not willing to come to Me that you may have life*" (John 5:39). If salvation could be obtained through only reading the Scriptures, then, logically, the Scriptures would have had to be available to every nation, tribe, peoples, and tongues throughout the ages. Even then, unless illiteracy was non-existent, not everyone would have had the opportunity to read and understand the love of

God and His saving grace. Therefore, *the breath of the Almighty makes available to every human an understanding and path to His love and guidance.*

Peter goes a step further to assure us that God's Divine grace contains all of the ingredients necessary for spiritual growth. At this point Peter introduces the journey through the seven characteristics of the divine nature of God. We are encouraged: *"giving all diligence, add to our faith virtue, to virtue knowledge, to knowledge self-control, to self-control perseverance, to perseverance godliness, to godliness brotherly kindness, and to brotherly kindness love" - the bond of perfection* (2 Peter 1:5-7).

To clarify, the seven characteristics of the Divine nature of God are: *Virtue, Knowledge, Self-control, Perseverance, Godliness, Brotherly Kindness, and Love.*

Beginning the Journey

To begin this glorious spiritual journey, Peter gives us the formula for guaranteed success. He tells us that we "have been given exceedingly great and precious promises, that through these [promises] you may be partakers of the divine nature, having escaped the corruption that is in the world through lust". (2 Peter 1:4) (In this context, "lust" is not exclusively sexual in nature as it encompasses all aspects of desire that influence a person to excesses.) Paul in a letter to his spiritual son, Titus, begins in this manner:

> Paul, a servant of God and an apostle of Jesus Christ, according to the faith of God's elect and the acknowledgement of the truth which is according to

godliness, in hope of eternal life which God, who cannot lie, promised before time began. Titus 1:1, 2

Peter says there are great and precious promises upon which our faith must hold fast. Let us now examine these promises, for they hold the key to partaking of the divine nature.

The *first* promise is powerful in its direct simplicity: *"being confident of this very thing, that He who has begun a good work in you will complete it until the day of Jesus Christ"* (Philippians 1:6). Only God can begin and complete His divine work in you. Thus, the confidence this promise brings should far outweigh any doubts that our human nature might advance. The Creator, who knows and understands all of our needs, is executing the plan of redemptive love exclusively for each individual.

The *second* promise gives greater illumination to the first:

Therefore, my beloved, as you have always obeyed not as in my presence only, but now much more in my absence, work out your own salvation with fear and trembling; for it is God who works in you both to will and to do for His good pleasure. Philippians 2:12, 13

Satan, or evil, the enemy of our souls, tries to convince us that while it may be one's intention to do God's will, it is impossible to actually succeed. Indeed, God does work in us the will, or desire, to please Him. But more importantly, He gives us the ability to *accomplish* His will. This dual action, to will and to do, speaks defeat to evil.

The *third* promise predates the world:

> Blessed be the God and Father of our Lord Jesus Christ, who has blessed us with every spiritual blessing in the heavenly places in Christ, just as He [Father] chose us in Him [Jesus] before the foundation of the world, that we should be holy and without blame before Him [Father] in love, having predestined us to adoption as sons by Jesus Christ to Himself [Father], according to the good pleasure of His [Father] will, to the praise of the glory of His grace, by which He has made us accepted in the Beloved [Jesus]. Ephesians 1:3-6

Before the foundation of the world, before religions came to be, *our Divine Father guaranteed eternal life to all who would accept Him*. This promise means that God at no time lost sight of His elects' destiny.

The *fourth* promise puts God's timetable into perspective:

> But beloved, do not forget this one thing, that with the Lord one day is as a thousand years, and a thousand years as one day. The Lord is not slack concerning His promise, as some count slackness, but is long suffering toward us, not willing that "any" should perish but that "all" should come to repentance. 2 Peter 3:8, 9

God's time keeping is not the same as ours. If God is not willing that any should be lost, it means that He leaves no stone unturned in trying to *draw* every individual in every age to "repentance", or, a loving relationship with Him. How comforting to know the degree of God's pro-activeness on behalf of our salvation.

Jesus Himself declares the *fifth* promise:

> "My sheep hear My voice, and I know them and they follow Me. And I give them eternal life, and they shall never perish; neither shall anyone snatch them out of My hand. My Father, who has given them to Me, is greater than all; and no one is able to snatch them out of My Father's hand. I and My Father are one." John 10:27-30

These *five promises* should be committed to memory and often recited:

1) *He will complete the transforming work He has started in us.*
2) *He will plant the will and desire to partake of His nature.*
3) *He has adopted us before the creation of the world.*
4) *He is long suffering and patiently awaits our repentance (or acknowledgement of error in thought or deed).*
5) *He promises eternal life in the protection of His hands.*

If our life is to be transformed as we become partakers of His divine nature, our faith must hold fast to these promises. The reward of being born again of the Holy Spirit is that we may have access to the power of the endless life. This miraculous moment occurs when our spirit intentionally aligns with the Holy Spirit. There are no doctrines or particular acts required by well-meaning religious groups that can substitute for this life changing experience. Failure to engage in this encounter with the Holy Spirit only assigns us to a place of disappointment and discouragement.

An analogy to the difficulty of attaining the higher spiritual life without Divine connection may be likened to the futility of trying to ascend a long *descending* escalator. Not only is it tiring and dangerous, but a momentary pause finds one back at the bottom, having to start all over again. God's promises suggest a different mode of ascension. Our Lord and Savior has designed and operates a divine elevator that we can enter through the doors of repentance and submission. The Divine Operator then begins the ascension from faith *to virtue to knowledge to self-control to perseverance to godliness to brotherly kindness and to love* as we ride the Divine elevator to the penthouse of God's majesty.

Chapter 11
Virtue

...if there is any virtue and if there is anything praiseworthy - meditate on these things.

Philippians 4:8

T he prerequisite for being partakers of the divine nature is to be born again in our spiritual being - heart, mind, and soul. We are then in a position to receive a portion of the very nature that Christ possessed when He defeated Satan at Calvary and rose to inherit from His Father all power in heaven and earth. Resting in the glorious state of submission enables the process of "being born again" possible. A precious gift awaits those who choose to allow God to build within them a *spiritual house*. Keep in mind Solomon's words: "unless the Lord builds the house, they labor in vain who build it" (Psalms 127:1). Peter articulates the process and results of this spiritual building:

> Coming to Him [Jesus] as to a living stone, rejected indeed by men, but chosen by God and precious, you also, as living stones are being built up a spiritual house, a holy priesthood, to offer up spiritual sacrifices acceptable to God through Jesus Christ. 1 Peter 2:4, 5

Jesus, the Rock of our salvation, was broken into innumerable precious stones at Calvary in order that God might use these divine materials to build a spiritual house within humanity - worthy to be inhabited by the Holy Spirit.

In spiritual numerology, seven represents perfection or completeness. Virtue is the first of the seven building stones. To understand its role, we will explore three definitions. The dictionary defines "virtue" as:

> "Moral excellence and righteousness; goodness."[8] In order to fully appreciate this definition, we need to observe some of its synonyms—morality, rectitude, uprightness, fidelity, loyalty, piety, efficacy, merit.[9]

Peter uses an interesting metaphor to describe the spiritual building process:

> Therefore, laying aside all malice, all guile, hypocrisy, envy, and all evil speaking, as newborn babes, desire the pure milk of the word, which you may grow thereby, if indeed you have tasted that the Lord is gracious. 1 Peter 2:1-3

The divine formula given by God is designed to produce spiritually healthy individuals. This formula is not only rich in divine nutrients but is delicious to the spiritual palate. This taste, once acquired, is essential, for it creates a desire for more of the formula.

---

[8]   "Virtue," *The American Heritage Dictionary*, 3rd ed. 1994

[9]   "Virtue," *Webster's Collegiate Thesaurus*, 1976 ed.

Oh, taste and see that the Lord is good; blessed is the man who trusts in him. Psalms 34:8

The second definition of virtue is biblical and comes to us from the Greek word *dunamis*, which means "miraculous power."[10] We have already witnessed that faith exhibited by the woman who, seeking a cure for a serious blood disease, secretly touched Jesus' garment as He passed through a crowd (see Chapter 3). The Word says that immediately Jesus knew within Himself that virtue (Dunamis) had gone out of Him (Luke 8:46). Jesus felt a power drain from His being since he possessed the full complement of divinity through the indwelling of the Holy Spirit. He instantly reacted to the powerful call of the woman's faith. As word went out about this miracle, many who heard sought to touch Him as well, and all who did were healed (Matthew 14:34-36).

Paul uses the third definition of virtue, the Greek word *arête*, meaning "excellence" or "praiseworthy".[11]

Finally, brethren, whatever things are true, whatever things are noble, whatever things that are just, whatever things are pure, whatever things are lovely, whatever things are of good report, if there is any virtue, and if there is anything praiseworthy—meditate on these things. Philippians 4:8

Meditation is a tremendous source of inspiration to one's spirit and its relative parts—heart, mind, and soul. Through meditation, we distance

---

10   Strong, *Dictionary of the Greek Testament*, 24.

11   Strong, *Dictionary of the Greek Testament*, 15.

ourselves from the ever-increasing activities of our lives, giving us serenity that allows our spirit to feed on eternal values. Paul is careful not to dictate specifically what we should meditate upon, but suggests whatever things are just, pure, lovely, and of good report, meditate on these things. Meditation not only inspires our being but also brings us a divine peace that transcends the temporal. In our busy world, we seem to have less and less time to meditate, robbing us of God's premiere avenue of communication. Isaiah intones, "You will keep him in perfect peace, whose mind is stayed on You, because he trusts in You" (Isaiah 26:3).

Chapter 12
Knowledge

For wisdom is a defense as money is a defense, but the excellence of knowledge is that wisdom gives life to those who have it.

Ecclesiastes 7:12

K nowledge is a word that virtually explodes with meaning. In the history of the world, knowledge has never been so readily available to so many people and in so many different media. The accumulation of knowledge available in books, television, and the internet staggers the imagination. In today's high-tech world, the acquisition of knowledge is not an option - it is a necessity. The youth of today are faced with challenges in the educational arena that hardly existed a few generations ago.

Let us keep in mind, Peter makes a clear distinction between earthly and divine knowledge. The knowledge available to us in libraries and on the internet constitutes the exploration and creative thinking of humans throughout the ages. This knowledge is important in that it equips us with societal skills and technical information necessary to succeed. On the other hand, divine knowledge, as referred to by Peter, deals with spiritual power that helps the individual as well as society to reach a higher standard of morality and ethical living. Solomon summates, "for the Lord gives wisdom; from His mouth come knowledge and understanding" (Proverbs 2:6). God provides us with knowledge and understanding through the *spirit within*. He is not limited by geography, language, or time in communicating His will to the world. This reality is important to keep in mind for it clarifies how people in the most remote parts of the world throughout the ages have had access to God's divine knowledge.

Several points are necessary to consider in order to understand the process of acquiring the divine nature. Firstly, *how does God gain knowledge about us?* David speaks directly to this question:

> Oh Lord, You have searched me and know me. You know my sitting down and my rising up; You understand my thought afar off. You comprehend my path and my lying down, and are acquainted with all my ways. For there is not a word on my tongue but behold, O Lord, You know it all together. You have hedged me behind and before, and laid your hand upon me. Such knowledge is too wonderful for me; it is high, I cannot attain it ... Search me, O god, and know my heart; try me, and know my anxieties; and see if there is any wicked in me, and lead me in the way everlasting. Psalm 139:1-6, 23, 24

Even the most honorable individuals can attest to evil thoughts and emotions from time to time, leaving them astonished at themselves. David's request to God to "search me" focuses on the importance of knowing one's true self. As we enter the glorious state of submission (surrender to God's love), we sense an overpowering need to know who we truly are.

Secondly, *what is God's will for us?* This question deserves our utmost attention, as it begs for an individual response. The personal nature of salvation requires God to prescribe a plan suitable for each individual. *"One plan fits all" is a widely sold concept that is dangerous to us on a soul level.*

This deceptive message, unfortunately, has been the cornerstone of many religious groups who have reduced salvation to a set of doctrines and rules particular to their own understandings. Any departure from these teachings, they further charge, may indeed terminate the individual's right to God's kingdom. Little wonder that Jesus exclaimed that those who promoted such deception were "teaching as doctrines the commandments of men" (Matthew 15:9). And He warned, "they are blind leaders of the blind. And if the blind leads the blind, both will fall into a ditch" (Matthew 15:14). To early believers, Paul intones a similar message: "beware lest anyone cheat you through philosophy and empty deceit, according to the tradition of men, according to the basic principles of the world, and not according to Christ". (Colossians 2:8)

When we realize the individual attention that God gives to each of us who seek His will, we are driven to foster a closer relationship with Him through prayer. Jesus, in teaching His disciples how to pray, incorporates the following words into the Lord's prayer: that "Your [God's] will be done on earth as it is in heaven" (Matthew 6:10). David, finding repentance from his sins, gives the following prayer:

> Hear my prayer, O Lord, give ear to my supplications! In Your faithfulness answer me, and in Your righteousness. Do not enter into judgment with Your servant, for in Your sight no one living is righteous ... Cause me to hear Your loving kindness in the morning, for in You do I trust; cause me to know the way in which I should walk, for I lift up my soul to You ... Teach me to do Your will, for You are my God; Your Spirit is good. Lead me   in the land of uprightness. Psalms 143:1, 2, 8, 10

As follows from David's prayer, three important verbs should be noted:

1) *To hear* God's voice
2) *To know* His way
3) *To do* His will

These verbs show response to the drawing of the Father, and more importantly, responsibility for action. Lest we forget, Jesus reminds us, in His Sermon on the Mount that we serve a God that has numbered the hairs of everyone's head, and not a sparrow falls that He is not mindful! David intones, "how precious also are Your thoughts to me, O God! How great is the sum of them! If I should count them, they would be more in number than the sand; when I awake, I am still with You" (Psalms 139:17, 18).

Thirdly, *how important is the knowledge of Jesus Christ and His teachings to our daily living?*

Attaining the knowledge of our Lord and Savior, Jesus Christ, is most precious. To be complete in Him speaks to a quality of life that far exceeds earthly riches and fame. It speaks to a high life that has not only earthly value, but eternal worth. When we look at the fragmentation of our daily lives caused by its vicissitudes and disappointments, the fact that we can obtain this completeness or cohesiveness should quicken our spirits and encourage us to seek this knowledge of Christ.

"That the God of our Lord Jesus Christ, the Father of Glory, may give to you the spirit of wisdom and revelation in the knowledge of Him, the eyes of your understanding being enlightened; that you may know what is the hope of His calling, what are the riches of the glory of His inheritance in the saints. Ephesians 1:17, 18

"For in Him dwells all the fullness of the Godhead bodily; and you are complete in Him, who is the head of all principality and power" (Colossians 2:9).

Chapter 13
Self-Control

...self-control. Against such there is no law.

Galatians 5:23

O f the seven divine characteristics, the third, self-control, is the one for which philosophical debate is mute. First and foremost, it is the control of self, not the control of others. Needless to say, virtually all of the organized religions have made controlling others the cornerstone of their teachings. *It is a sad commentary when the power of deception leads an individual to feel safer when being controlled by another's thoughts than when one's self is guided by the Spirit.*

Why does "*self*" need control? Paul in his great soliloquy on the condition of humanity gives the answer: "because the carnal mind is enmity against God; for it is not subject to the law of God, nor indeed can be. So then, those who are in the flesh cannot please God" (Romans 8:7, 8). To my mind, there can be no argument on this point.

Humankind's inhumanity speaks volumes. Our cries of astonishment are multiplied when we see even children murdering children at will. We need self-control because we inherit traits, we learn by example, and are influenced by our environment. Finally, we must fight pride, arrogance, and self - aggrandizement.

To begin finding a solution to the problems associated with self-control, let us recall two of our divine promises. First, "being confident of this very thing, that He who has begun a good work in you will complete it until the day of Jesus Christ" (Philippians 1:6). Second, "for it is God who works in you both to will and to do for His good pleasure". (Philippians 2:13) Our complex natures clearly require divine solutions. Why do both Peter and Paul call it self-control when clearly it is God who has to control us? The answer is simple: *self-control is really God-control when self chooses to submit.* And remember, *submission* is an issue of choice. James articulates this point: "He gives more grace. Therefore, He says; 'God resists the proud, but gives grace to the humble.' Therefore, submit to God. Resist the devil and he will flee from you" (James 4:6, 7).

When we submit (surrender in faith) to God, the devil is not fleeing from us but from the divine nature of which we are now partakers. *In other words, he is fleeing from God in us.* Submission to God means having direct access to experiencing His love. There is no greater comfort, strength and hope than to know that one is loved by God. We are then able to hurdle all of life's obstacles knowing that "all things work together for good to those who love God" (Romans 8:28).

The concept of self-control involves more than meets the eye. *The active ingredient in self-control is humility,* which leads to peace, the very peace that Jesus gave to His disciples when He was leaving the earth and continues to give to all who submit to His will. Jesus says: "peace I leave with you, My peace I give to you; not as the world gives do I give to you. Let not your heart be troubled, neither let it be afraid" (John 14:27). Again, He says, "these things I have spoken to you, that in Me you may have peace. In the world you will have tribulation; but be of good cheer, I have overcome the world" (John 16:33). Not idle word!

A short time later, while Jesus was being abused on His way to Calvary in a manner that breaks our hearts each time we read it, we are stunned that in the midst of this abuse, "He held His peace" (Matthew 26:63).[12] If you do not have peace, it cannot be held, for you cannot hold what you do not have. This was the ultimate test and demonstration of how self-control works in real time and under real circumstances. Paul elucidates on the question of peace through Jesus:

> But now in Christ Jesus you who once were far off have been made near by the blood of Christ. For He Himself is our peace, who has made both one, and has broken down the middle wall of division between us ... Now, therefore, you are no longer strangers and foreigners, but fellow citizens with the saints and members of the household of God, having been built on the foundation of the apostles and prophets, Jesus Christ Himself being the chief cornerstone, in whom the whole building, being joined together, grows into a holy temple in the Lord, in whom you also are being built together for a habitation of God in the Spirit. Ephesians 2:13, 14, 19-22

Through faith, we understand the power that Jesus had to defeat Satan. That same power is available to the partakers of His divine nature. Let us join with Paul in saying:

---

12   *The Holy Bible*, King James Version, (Nashville: Thomas Nelson Publishers, 1976).

Rejoice in the Lord always. Again, I will say rejoice! Let your gentleness be known to all men. The Lord is at hand. Be anxious for nothing, but in everything by prayer and supplication, with thanksgiving, let your requests be made to God; and the peace of God, which surpasses all understanding, will guard your hearts and minds through Christ Jesus." Philippians 4:4-7

When you are at peace with God, you are at peace with yourself. When you are at peace with yourself, you are at peace with the world.

Chapter 14
Perseverance

And take the helmet of salvation, and the sword of the Spirit, which is the word of God; praying always with all prayer and supplication in the Spirit, being watchful to this end with all perseverance and supplication for all the saints.

Ephesians 6:17, 18

L ife is not a sprint, it is a daily race of great endurance. No one was better equipped to understand this than Peter. His journey represents a "test case" of perseverance that exemplifies how we can each be partakers of the divine nature. As his time on earth was coming to an end, Peter, the first disciple called by Jesus, confirmed that there can be life-changing victory in Christ. During these last hours, a multitude of memories must have flooded his spirit. Peter remembered his daily bout with fear and the disappointment that caused him to deny his Lord not once but three times. He also remembered the many hardships that befell him; beatings, prison, being ship-wrecked, and finally the brutal persecution leading to his death.

Notwithstanding his tribulations, Peter's memories are not all depressing. With joy he recalled the many healings, the raising of the dead, and most of all Pentecost, which gave him the power to preach the wonderful gospel to all who would listen, be they Jew or Gentile.

Divine perseverance is the ability to endure difficulties, obstacles, and unforeseen dilemmas, while not losing faith in God. Paul also described his desire for the heavenly life and shared these comforting thoughts:

For we know that if our earthly house, this tent, is destroyed, we have a building from God, a house not made with hands, eternal in the heavens...Now he who has prepared us for this very thing is God, who also has given us the Spirit as a guarantee. 2 Corinthians 5:1, 5

What could be more consoling in a long and arduous journey than to be guaranteed that it was not in vain. Here again, we see the Holy Spirit at work with our spirit to ensure our success. Paul reiterates to the church of Ephesus that the work of the Holy Spirit is not only to guarantee an inheritance but to seal us with its promise. Paul states:

> ...in Him you also trusted, after you heard the word of truth, the gospel of your salvation; in whom also, having believed, you were sealed with Holy Spirit of promise, who is the guarantee of our inheritance until the redemption of the purchased possession, to the praise of His glory.
> Ephesians 1:13, 14

There can be no perseverance without another important word - hope. Peter articulates:

> Blessed be the God and Father of our Lord Jesus Christ, who according to His abundant mercy has begotten us again to a living hope through the resurrection of Jesus Christ from the dead, to an inheritance incorruptible and undefiled and that does not fade away, reserved in heaven for you, who are kept by the power of God through faith for salvation ready to be revealed in the last time. In this you greatly rejoice, though now for a little while, if need be, you have been

grieved by various trials, that the genuineness of your faith, being much more precious than gold   that perishes, though it is tested by fire, may be found to praise, honor, and glory at the revelation of Jesus Christ. 1 Peter 1:3-7

Paul, in writing to Titus, further strengthens this living hope when he says: 'in hope of eternal life which God, who cannot lie, promised before time began" (Titus 1:2). As if being sealed and guaranteed is not enough for our faith to grasp, he reminds us that our inheritance was promised *before time began* and that *God cannot lie.*

In a letter to the church in Rome, Paul creates an interesting cause-and-effect scenario by stating:

> Therefore, having been justified by faith, we have peace with God through our Lord Jesus Christ, through whom also we have access by faith into this grace in which we stand, and rejoice in hope of the glory of God. And not only that, but we also glory in tribulations, knowing that tribulation produces perseverance; and perseverance, character; and character, hope. Now hope does not disappoint, because the love of God has been poured out in our hearts by the Holy Spirit who was given to us. Romans 5:1-5

The writer of Hebrews encourages us to run the race by reminding us that God is not unjust and will not forget our labors on His behalf, and *hope is an anchor for the soul.* (Hebrews 6) And Paul reminds us that we must run the race as one who intends to win, not with uncertainty, but with resolve. (1

Corinthians 9:14-16) The hope that lives in us, coupled with the sealing and guarantee of eternal life, is what makes divine perseverance a must. *With tha. great cloud of witnesses who have gone before, we are called to be long distance runners.*

Therefore I exhort first of all that supplications, prayers, intercessions, and giving of thanks be made for all men, for kings and all who are in authority, that we may lead a quiet and peaceable life in all godliness and reverence.

1 Timothy 2:1, 2

To partake of the divine nature does not mean that we become little gods. Rather, that we reflect the beauty and glory of divinity, and the source of this beauty is shared with others. Peter calls Godliness the exhibition of Christ's character. Understandably, *the power of virtue, the knowledge of God's will, the submission to Him for self-control, and the perseverance should result in godliness seen in us.* But, make no mistake, this quality is not acquired by any goodness in us, in fact Paul calls it the "mystery of godliness" and gives us a condensed version of how it became possible. Paul states: "and without controversy great is the mystery of godliness: God was manifested in the flesh, justified in the Spirit, seen by angels, preached among the Gentiles, believed on in the world, received up in glory". (1 Timothy 3:16)

John explains this mystery of godliness and how we receive it by stating 'as many as received Him [Jesus], to them He gave the right to become children of God, even to those who believe in His name" who were born, not of blood, nor of the will of the flesh, nor of the will of man, but of God". (John 1:12, 13)

Paul, who experienced counterfeit examples of godliness warns us about false teachers. This warning was true then and remains true today:

> Now the Spirit expressly says that in latter times some will depart from the faith, giving heed to deceiving spirits and doctrines of demons, speaking lies in hypocrisy, having their own conscience seared with a hot iron, forbidding to marry, and commanding to abstain from foods which God created to be received with thanksgiving by those who believe and know the truth. For every creature of God is good, and nothing is to be refused if it is received with thanksgiving; for it is sanctified by the word of God and prayer. Timothy 4:1-5

Paul warns that deception comes in many forms, not only in restrictive living:

> But know this, that in the last days perilous times will come: For men will be lovers of themselves, lovers of money, boasters, proud, blasphemers, disobedient to parents, unthankful, unholy, unloving, unforgiving, slanderers, without self-control, brutal, despisers of good, traitors, headstrong, haughty, lovers of pleasure rather than lovers of God, having a form of godliness but denying its power. And from such people turn away! For of this sort are those who creep into households and make captives of gullible women loaded down with sins, led away by various lusts, always learning and never able to come to the knowledge of the truth. 2 Timothy 3:1-7

It is hard to believe that these deceptions could have a "form of godliness."

The religious world is filled with teachings that run the gamut of "do's and don'ts", all in an effort to produce a people that are fashioned after *humanity's* perception of godliness. Paul continues, "reject profane and old wives' fables, and exercise yourself rather to godliness. For bodily exercise profits a little, but godliness is profitable for all things, having promise of the life that now is and of that which is to come" (1 Timothy 4:7, 8).

Solomon brings this breadth of life and living into clear focus. He states:

> To everything there is a season, A time for every purpose
> under heaven:
> A time to be born, and a time to die;
> A time to plant, and a time to pluck what is planted;
> A time to kill, and a time to heal;
> A time to break down, and a time to build up;
> A time to weep, and a time to laugh;
> A time to mourn, and a time to dance;
> A time to cast away stones, and a time to gather stones;
> A time to embrace, and a time to refrain from embracing;
> A time to gain, and a time to lose;
> A time to keep, a time to throw away;
> A time to tear, and a time to sew;
> A time to keep silence, and a time to speak;
> A time to love, and a time to hate;
> A time of war, and a time of peace.

What profit has the worker from that in which he labors? I have seen the God-given task with which the sons of men are to be occupied. He has made everything beautiful in its time. Also, He has put eternity in their hearts, except no one can find out the work that God does from beginning to end. I know that there is nothing better for them than to rejoice, and to do good in their lives, and also that every man should eat and drink and enjoy the good of all his labor - it is the *gift* of God. Ecclesiastes 3:1-13

Some religions preach a prescribed fashion of living, while readily speaking about the gift of salvation, the gift of grace, and the gift of eternal life. But rarely, if ever, do they preach about the *gift of the good life here on earth Solomon clearly indicates that the secret to the good life is moderation in all things and a conscious appreciation for all of God's blessings.* To live in this godly manner is surely a gift. Godliness and contentment go hand in hand. Where godliness reigns there is peace and gentleness. Paul comments:

If anyone teaches otherwise and does not consent to wholesome words, even the words of our Lord Jesus Christ, and to the doctrine which is according to godliness, he is proud knowing nothing, but is obsessed with disputes and arguments over words, from which come envy, strife, reviling, evil suspicions, useless wranglings of men of corrupt minds and destitute of the truth, who suppose that godliness is a means of gain. From such withdraw yourself. But godliness with contentment is great gain. 1 Timothy 6:3-6

Godliness transcends culture, status, race, or any categorization that religions may choose to impose. Paul concludes with this powerful statement:

But I rejoiced in the Lord greatly that now at last your care for me has flourished again; though you surely did care, but you lacked opportunity. Not that I speak in regard to need, for I have learned in whatever state I am, to be content: I know how to be abased, and I know how to abound. Everywhere and in all things I have learned both to be full and to be hungry, both to abound and to suffer need. I can do all things through Christ who strengthens me.   Philippians 4:10-13

Godly living renders the enemy of our souls helpless. Not only does he flee from God's presence in us but is reminded that at the close of earth's history he must answer the summons of the Judge of the universe. Peter leaves us with a marvelous statement to strengthen our faith and speak peace to our souls in this present world, "the Lord knows how to deliver the godly out of temptations and to reserve the unjust under punishment for the day of judgment" (2 Peter 2:9).

Chapter 16
Brotherly Kindness

Honor all people. Love the brotherhood. Fear God. Honor the king.

1 Peter 2:17

T he seven divine attributes can be grouped into two categories. *Virtue, knowledge, self-control,* and *perseverance* could be labeled as attributes that deal with personal growth. *Godliness, brotherly kindness,* and *love,* however, go outside our personal sphere and globally encompass our relationship with the world. Adopting a perspective that reaches beyond a personal agenda demonstrates the genuineness of our spiritual growth. At this point our growth in Christ explodes in its divine power and manifests itself in the greatest form possible—brotherly kindness. However, one of the saddest commentaries, is that Christians, and other religious organizations, have often been at the forefront of racism and gender discrimination throughout the history of the world. Not only have many religious observers not practiced brotherly kindness, they have often spearheaded wars, massacres, and ethnic cleansings. Based on so many blatant inconsistencies, many rational thinking people reject religion and agree with Karl Marx that religion is "the opiate of the masses." These contradictions in religious agendas is causing individuals to miss out on the beauty of God's kindness.

The practice of brotherly kindness, if not genuine, soon turns to condescension on the part of the practitioner and resentment on the part of the recipient. Given time, they both grow further apart, with deep malevolent feelings toward each other. Unfortunately, the lack of brotherly kindness is not new to the people of God. When Moses' two sons were brought to him in the desert by his wife Zapora, and her father Jethro, Miriam and Aaron began to criticize and speak against Moses. They were angry at Moses because he had married an Ethiopian woman. Not only did they criticize him, but subsequently challenged his position as a prophet of God. Racism is an insidious evil that clouds our judgment on many issues. The root of racism is unbridled pride. It causes us to see ourselves as superior to others, using physical or cultural differences as justification. It would seem in this scenario that Miriam displeased God the most. As a prophetess and one who should have known better, she was struck with leprosy by God and thrown out of the camp for seven days (Numbers 12:1-16).

The problem of discrimination was also brought to Peter in a vision, which depicted all kinds of creatures on a great sheet bound at four corners descending towards him from heaven. He was ordered by God to kill the animals and eat. Peter, following the strict Jewish dietary laws, refused to eat, explaining that he had never eaten anything common or unclean. The Lord spoke a second time and declared "what God has cleansed you must not call common" (Acts 10:15). As Peter was pondering the meaning of this vision, a Roman Centurion named Cornelius, a just and righteous man, requested Peter to come and preach to him. When Peter arrived at his home, Cornelius said to him:

"Four days ago, I was fasting until this hour; and at the ninth hour I prayed in my house, and behold, a man stood before me in bright clothing, and said, 'Cornelius, your prayer has been heard, and your alms are remembered in the sight of God. Send therefore to Joppa and call Simon here, whose surname is Peter. He is lodging in the house of

Simon, a tanner, by the sea. When he comes, he will speak to you.' So I sent to you immediately, and you have done well to come. Now therefore, we are all present before God, to hear all the things commanded you by God. Then Peter opened his mouth and said; In truth I perceive that God shows no partiality. But in every nation, whoever fears Him and works righteousness is accepted by Him." Acts 10:30-35

Clearly, racism is but one of the ways in which humanity is called to condemn partiality. If impartiality is to be the norm for humanity, then we must face head on such demonic expressions as ethnic cleansing, racism, sexism, homophobia, and other forms of discrimination. As with all whose *spirit within* respond to the divine Spirit, we are called to be mediators of divine kindness and impartiality at the levels of home, community and the world. The clarion call of the prophet Amos is heard. "Let justice roll down like water, and righteousness like a mighty stream" (Amos 5:24).

James calls all humanity to demonstrate brotherly love and to renounce any form of discrimination in community life when he says:

My brethren, do not hold the faith of our Lord Jesus Christ, the Lord of glory, with partiality. For if there should come into your assembly a man with gold rings, in fine apparel, and there should also come in a poor man in filthy clothes, and you pay attention to the one wearing the fine clothes and say to him, "you sit here in a good place," and say to the poor man, "you stand there," or, "sit here at my foot stool," have you not shown partiality among yourselves and become judges with evil thoughts? If you really fulfill the royal law according to the Scripture, "you shall love you neighbor as yourself," you do well; but if you show partiality, you commit sin, and are convicted by the law as transgressors. James 2:1-4, 8, 9

The church is not the only place where partiality is practiced. The home is often a hotbed of discrimination and partiality, particularly with regard to the attitudes of some parents toward their children. Jacob displayed partiality when he clearly chose Joseph as his favorite son. By making his son a spectacle with "the coat of many colors", Jacob's partiality only helped to make Joseph a target of hatred by his other brothers (Genesis 37:1-4). As parents we cannot succumb to partiality, since the damage that this evil promotes can cause irreparable suffering. Concomitantly, the relationship between husband and wife should be an example of reciprocal divine kindness, setting an atmosphere that makes any form of discrimination or partiality within the home extinct.

The words of Paul to the Philippians ring true: "let nothing be done through selfish ambition or conceit, but in lowliness of mind let each esteem others better than himself. Let each of you look out not only for his own interests, but also for the interests of others" (Philippians 2:3, 4). Those who demonstrate the attribute of brotherly kindness can make strides in healing the wounds of the individual, the home, the community and the world. The inclusiveness and impartiality that form the cornerstone of brotherly kindness create leadership that is divinely guided.

Chapter 17
Love

He brought me to the banqueting house, and His banner over me was Love.

Song of Solomon 2:4

We come at last to the pinnacle of God's character—*love*. In reality, this love is more than just one of God's attributes; it is the very definition of His divine being. Unless we are born of the Spirit, any attempt on our part can only manufacture a pretense of this divine love. Paul, in a letter to the Colossians, beautifully places love in the context of all the other attributes of God. Paul states:

> Therefore, as the elect of God, holy and beloved, put on tender mercies, kindness, humbleness of mind, meekness, longsuffering; bearing with one another, and forgiving one another, if anyone has a complaint against another; even as Christ forgave you, so you also must do. But above all these things put on love, which is the bond of perfection. Colossians 3:12-14

The word "bond" so aptly describes love, for it unites all of the seven attributes together into one glorious union. One of the greatest demonstrations of God's love was displayed to Peter after he so blatantly denied Christ—not long before the Savior's journey to Calvary. Following the resurrection, Christ appeared incognito to Peter and six other disciples after they had fished all night with no success. He instructed them where to place their nets, helping them catch an abundance of fish. He later reveals Himself to Peter as the risen Christ and asks:

"Simon [Peter], Son of Jonah, do you love Me more than these?" He said to Him, "Yes, Lord; You know that I love you." He said to him, "Feed my lambs." He said to him again a second time, "Simon, Son of Jonah, do you love Me?" He said to Him, "Yes, Lord; You know that I love you." He said to him, "Tend my sheep." He said to him the third time, "Simon, Son of Jonah, do you love me?" Peter was grieved because he said to him the third time, "Do you love Me?" And he said to Him, "Lord, you know all things; you know that I love you." Jesus said to him, "Feed My sheep." John 21:15-17

Poetic justice is being exhibited when Jesus ask Peter *three times* if he loves Him - the same number of times that Peter had denied Him earlier. In this text, Christ further tries to show Peter that God's love is ubiquitous - it reaches out to every generation, from young to old.

First, He says, "Feed my lambs," referring both to young people as well as those who are "babes" in the Word. He then says, "Tend my sheep," referring to special care for all the needs of His people. Finally, He says, "Feed my sheep," referring to teaching the word of life to all the flock.

Though not apparent in the English translation, the Greek text of this passage uses different words for love. First, Jesus asks Peter, "do you love me more than these?" Peter responds "You know I love you." The verb used love first by Jesus, is *agapaō*.

In answering Jesus, Peter uses the verb for love, *phileo*. This exchange between Jesus and Peter gives us opportunity to explore the meaning of divine love. Let us first begin with Peter's response, and consider his usage of the verb *phileo*, for love. It means "to be a friend, or to be fond of an individual or an object, or having affection or personal attachment as a matter of sentiment or feeling."[13] This definition is completely understandable to the human mind. This love, based on affection, sentiment or feeling has been experienced at one time or another by all humanity. Further, this love can even be directed toward objects. Certainly, this love is a credible and powerful emotion that elicits deep feelings. However, an ever-present problem is associated with such love. Because emotions serve as the foundation for *phileo* love, being hurt, disappointed, or offended can cause sentiments to change, e.g., one falls in or out of love.

Divine love, or the *agape*, while it may appear similar, is fundamentally based on a different premise. A careful study of the *agape's* definition is most insightful in comprehending the love of God. *Agape* is defined as "embracing especially the judgment, and the deliberate assent of the will, as a matter of principal, duty and propriety."[14] Let us dissect this definition.

Firstly, regarding the statement, "Embracing especially the judgment...", the term 'judgment' refers to the application of justice. God declares that only He can sit in judgment, because only He is truly just. Secondly, continuing, the statement "...the deliberate assent of the will...." Refers to the understanding that when God, possessing all power and all wisdom gives assent or agreement to His will, no force in the universe can alter or deter the

---

13 Strong, *Dictionary of Greek Testament,* 75.

14 Strong, *Dictionary of the Greek Testament,* 76.

completion of His plans. Finally, "...as a matter of principle, duty and propriety...." declares the fact that the assent of His will is further bolstered by divine principle, guaranteed by unerring duty and performed with gracious propriety. Meaning, *the recipient of this divine love need have no fear of disappointment or loss, or changes of emotion.* John, in commenting on divine love, confirms this point, "there is no fear in love" (1 John 4:18).

Now, let us return to the conversation between Jesus and Peter. Twice Jesus uses the verb *agapaō* and twice Peter responds with the verb *phileo*. The third time Jesus asks Peter, "do you love me?" This time Jesus uses *phileo* to match Peter's responses. I would submit that this is not accidental on the part of Jesus. Though the Lord urgently desires Peter to experience *agape*, He realizes that Peter has yet to comprehend and internalize the deeper meaning of His divine love. So, Jesus meets Peter "where he is" spiritually by speaking in terms he could understand in that moment. Peter required the all-consuming experience of the "upper room" at Pentecost, when his life was transformed, to begin to understand *agape*. So, transforming would this love be, that in Peter's case his very shadow, like his Lord's, would later heal the sick. We can see God's patience exhibited as He took Peter where he was in his understanding of the human *phileo*, knowing that not long from then, Peter would experience the divine *agape* and "feed the flock."

Though Peter was annoyed by Jesus' persistence, the warmth and caring of the *agape* dissolved Peter's defenses and opened the floodgates to the healing process in his life. Paul in his letter to the Corinthians (1 Corinthians 13:1-8) clarifies that the greatest amount of faith and virtues are really nothing more than sounding brass and clanging symbols without the *agape*. A listing of the things that his love does and does not do is revealing:

Love does not envy
Love does not parade itself
Love is not puffed up or arrogant
Love does not behave rudely
Love does not seek its own or is selfish
Love is not provoked
Love does not think evil
Love does not rejoice in iniquity

On each of these points, volumes could be written and the spiritual mind can find much to ponder. Of the things that love is, we find the following:

Love rejoices in the truth
Love bears all things
Love believes all things
Love hopes in all things
Love endures all things
Love suffers long and is kind
Love never fails

These seven points of *agape* make human love pale by comparison. All those of the past, present, and future who partake of *agape,* experience a foretaste of the power of the endless divine life.

Religious groups promote many outward manifestations that are designed to show the world that they are disciples of God. But Jesus gives only one sign that is proof beyond doubt. Jesus says, "a new commandment I give to you, *that you love one another; as I have loved you*, that you also love one another. By this all will know that you are My disciples, if you have love for on another" (John 13:34, 35). *The litmus test of love for all humanity.*

From the foundation of the world, God reserved this *agape* for His adopted heirs throughout the ages. John's vision of diverse peoples intoning a united cry of joy for their salvation, confirms beyond a shadow of a doubt that God the Father and His Son the Creator, are more than able through the Holy Spirit to bring to the *spirit within* all power and grace.

Chapter 18
Final Reflections

W hen Solomon declared that life should be lived to the fullest, with joy and thanksgiving, and that, more importantly, it was a gift from God, he encapsulated the purpose and efficacy of the spirit within. To live a life pleasing to God, rewarding to ourselves, and to accept the gift of salvation, is not only the will of God, it is the total preoccupation of divinity.

The purpose of this inquiry has been to convey the commitment that God the Father made, before the foundation of the world, to draw all humanity to experience the love and saving power of His Son Jesus, through the indwelling of the Holy Spirit. The immeasurable love of God, expressed in the manifestation of the Word made flesh who dwelt among us, speaks to our hearts through the mystical power of faith - that power that explores the essence of divinity and draws us to seek the gift of repentance and wholeheartedly embrace the glorious state of submission to Him.

Through the spirit, God's lamp, he illuminates the content of our hearts, exposes the intent of our minds, and inscribes His inspiration in our souls. This quartet of our mystical essence - spirit, heart, mind, and soul—when tuned by the Holy Spirit, sings here on earth His heavenly refrain that inspires humanity and causes the universe to rejoice. The inspiration of the Almighty imparts His divine nature to us in the form of His character traits: virtue, knowledge, self-control, perseverance, godliness, brotherly kindness, and love, which means that our life on this earth has the potential to be rich in love, peace, thanksgiving, and worship.

The enemy of our souls, Satan, or evil, is no match for the imparted power of divinity. As Paul so aptly put it, "Yet in all these things, we are more than conquerors, through Him who loved us." (Romans 8:37) And indeed, "If God is for us, who can be against us?" (Romans 8:31) Surely the grace that flows from Calvary, grace that is greater than our sins, makes life not only worth living but ensures that our eternity has already begun.

My fervent prayer is that the reader will respond to the drawing of the Father as He welcomes us to our eternal home. Let us join Paul in his resolve when he says, "for I am persuaded that neither death nor life, nor angels nor principalities nor powers, nor things present nor things to come, nor height nor depth, nor any other created thing, shall be able to separate us from the love of God which is in Christ Jesus our Lord" (Romans 8:38, 39).

About The Author

Dr. Jon Robertson pastored the California based Facts of Faith Christian Fellowship for fourteen years. With his congregation, he explored the enriching power of God's love and the mysteries of His saving grace. *The Spirit Within* emanates from that enriching and rewarding experience.

In addition to his pastoral duties and inspiring motivational presentations, Dr. Robertson is an accomplished musician, holding a Doctorate of Musical Arts degree from the Juilliard School in New York City. He is also the recipient of two Honorary Doctorates in Humane Letters. For thirty-four years, he was the Conductor and Music Director of the Redlands Symphony in Redlands, California. He has guest-conducted orchestras nationally and internationally and has been a participant in numerous summer music festivals around the world.

As an academician, Dr. Robertson was the Chair of the Oakwood University Department of Music, The Thayer Conservatory of Music and Chair of the Department of Music and Professor of Conducting at the Herb Alpert School of Music at The University of California, Los Angeles (UCLA). Since 2005, Dr. Robertson is the Dean of the Lynn University Conservatory of Music in Boca Raton, Florida.

Dr. Robertson is the co-founder of Foundation Espoir (Haiti, 1995), Foundation Hope for Haiti (US, 2002), and Village of Vision for Haiti/Foundation Enfant Jésus (US, 2004). He is a spiritual and musical advisor to people of all ages.

Made in the USA
Columbia, SC
01 May 2024

35110855R00063